Making the Grade

This book is lovingly dedicated to the memory
of Vivienne Litt. I consider Vivienne one of
the most important mentors on my
educational journey. Without her, obtaining
my Ph.D. would not have been possible.

To all the people with learning disabilities,
especially to those who have not had
the support and advantages
that I have had through the years.

To the teachers and parents who,
with patience, love, and skill,
work to make a difference
for children, adolescents, and adults.

Contents

Acknowledgments

I value the support of my mother, Dorothy Upham; my sisters, Diane Fisk and Debra Holdsworth; and Aunt Helen d'Italia, who made me laugh and encouraged me to share my story. I want to thank my adopted family, Becky, Jon, and Gwen, who tolerated me and delayed important events so that I could meet my self-imposed deadlines. Many friends have supported me during the writing of this book—especially, Pat, Marlene, Vivian, and Steve.

Dayle Upham

Many people helped make this book possible. Without the support of my family (three children, four grandchildren), it could never have been completed. For invaluable assistance in the reading of the manuscript and the suggestions that followed, I want to thank my sister, Beth Hardesty; my graduate student, Karolyn Carpenter, who read and reacted to each chapter of the work in progress; Keene State College's past vice president for academic affairs, Gordon Leversee, who saw to it that I was awarded a sabbatical leave to work on the manuscript; and Dean Ann Waling, who was supportive throughout the project. Many students and teachers read parts of the manuscript and provided their support and constructive criticism; to all of them I say, "Thank you." I especially want to thank my friend and expert editor, Sally Pore, for the thoroughness with which she read each chapter, edited, and provided invaluable suggestions.

Ginny Trumbull

Introduction

The little girl entered school with enthusiasm and excitement about finally reaching the first grade. She would soon be reading books just like her older sister, writing letters to Grandma, and discovering all the secrets of the world around her. She had been the leader among her preschool friends; both boys and girls wanted her to join their groups. The first week of first grade was great—just what she had imagined. Then came the second week, when her classmates began to learn the letters of the alphabet with their corresponding sounds, and how to combine them to read. The little girl didn't understand what was going on. The squiggles on the page, the sounds they made, and the words read when several squiggles were put together made no sense at all.

Every day, schoolwork grew harder. She didn't understand how the other kids had learned to read and write! She stopped being the leader and began to feel left out. She didn't want the teacher to call on her to read because she couldn't do it. She refused to try and finally the teacher stopped calling on her. Sometimes, she worked alone with the teacher after school; but she still couldn't solve the mystery of reading and writing. She decided to skip school once in a while, and sit and watch the men building a house across the street from the school. When the construction workers ate lunch, she opened her lunch bag from home and ate too. When school was over and her classmates reappeared, she walked home at the right time.

As she grew older, the little girl fell farther and farther behind her classmates. She tried to be good in school so everyone would like her, but she could never seem to satisfy anyone. Sometimes, she became so angry that she would beat up another child. The more she hurt the child, the better she felt. She could prove her strength by beating someone up—at least she could do something well.

1

Her teachers and her parents didn't know what to do. They decided she was simply "slow" and that it would help if she repeated a grade. But staying back didn't help at all; instead, the girl just felt dumb, and believed she was being punished for not learning as quickly as the other children. She never seemed to do anything "smart" like her sister or her friends. When she finally went on to junior and senior high, she found that the one thing she could do well was play sports. She was an excellent field hockey and softball player. So she focused on sports, but even that backfired. Without good grades, she couldn't remain on the team! She really wanted to graduate from high school so that she could find a job that didn't require reading and writing. But she knew she would never graduate if she couldn't improve her grades. What was the use of trying to succeed at anything? She was just a "loser."

MAKING THE GRADE: THE BOOK

This book is based on the reflections of Dayle, now in her fifties, who describes herself as the little girl who entered school with enthusiasm. Today, many teachers and parents would recognize her learning disability because of her problems with reading and writing. However, when Dayle was in elementary and secondary school, few people knew about learning disabilities, or *dyslexia*, which in the medical definition is the inability to read or write well. Today, educators are far more familiar with these problems, but that awareness hasn't always led to solutions. According to the U.S. Department of Education (1991), approximately 4 percent of the school-age population (48 percent of students with all disabilities) have one or more learning disabilities. Most of these students suffer academically as well as vocationally. Perhaps most devastating of all are the psychosocial and emotional ramifications of a learning disability. Dayle, as the opening story describes, suffered from both.

In this book, we have attempted to tell Dayle's story, in her own words. She has recorded her memories of academic and social problems throughout her school and employment years. Each reflection exhibits dramatic examples of her disability and is a strong statement about how it feels to be learning disabled. A commentary follows each reflection. Strategies drawn from Dayle's writings and the experiences of both authors have been developed for approaching each of the problems described by Dayle. Strategies based on strengths, such as using visual maps and developing support systems, are among the teaching procedures suggested. Since there is growing evidence that a focus on remediating weaknesses is ineffective, the underlying theme of this book is the building of coping skills based on an individual's strengths.

We can learn a great deal from Dayle. She has proved many times that the warning of a fifth-grade teacher was grossly incorrect: "You'll be lucky if you can be more than a garbage collector." Now, having completed her Ph.D. in special education, Dayle has far exceeded the expectations of the teacher. She has experienced failure in school and in employment situations, but she has always found the inner strength to keep going.

What is that strength? How did she find it? What strategies did she develop to help her cope with other people's reactions to her disability? In this text, Dayle addresses many of those questions. Her descriptions of her learning disabilities are vivid. She communicates very directly not only how a learning disability appears to the outsider, but also how it feels to the individual who has the disability.

Dayle is not identical to any other student with a learning disability. Like many, she has significant language and cognitive processing problems that interfere with several skill areas important for successful learning, but her particular pattern of learning is unique to her. She has her own style of learning, as does everyone. As researchers and practitioners agree, dyslexia is a heterogeneous disability (Mercer, 1993; Lerner, 1993; Bos and Vaughn, 1994) and individuals with learning disabilities exhibit a variety of behaviors and characteristics (NJCLD, 1988). Along with the differences, however, there are many experiences and feelings that children and adults with learning disabilities share. Anyone with personal experience with a learning disability recognizes that person's struggles in Dayle's reflections. There are both similarities and differences between Dayle's ways of learning and those of others. As an example, Dayle has an excellent memory for visual events and is strong in math, but she has poor generalization skills and reads with great difficulty. Another person with learning disabilities may have a poor visual memory and be weak in math, yet generalize well and be a strong reader. Indeed, the many faces of learning disabilities make them an enigma to those who try so hard to help individuals affected find successful strategies for learning and living.

Medical and educational literature list theories about learning disabilities, their causes, and approaches for overcoming them in abundance. Since the term was created in 1963 to subsume conditions known as perceptual handicaps, dyslexia, word blindness, minimal brain dysfunction, and others, researchers have continued to attempt to determine exactly what neurological and/or environmental differences exist in the lives of the individual with a learning disability. Brain studies are leading to promising answers and many educational approaches seem feasible in certain cases. But there are still many unanswered questions about these disabilities. We do know that this is a heterogeneous disability in that it comes in many forms and levels of severity. Even the definition provided by the Department of Education for coding purposes is vague. The teacher and parent of a child with learning disabilities knows well that it can affect oral or written language, reading, math, spatial orientation, or social interactions. Educators also know that there is no one remediation technique that works effectively with everyone who has a learning disability.

Not only do experts disagree on what constitutes a learning disability, they also disagree on how to evaluate effectively students with a suspected disability and what to do about it once it has been diagnosed. In many school systems, an inordinate number of students are identified as learning disabled due partially to the fact that the definition lacks specificity. This makes evaluation problematic at best. Students who are difficult to teach and do not seem to fall into any of the more easily defined categories of special education (hearing impaired, physically disabled, speech impaired) are often considered to be learning disabled because they look and act normal and appear to have more options and a greater chance of achieving success than students who are identified with other disabilities.

The large number of students identified with learning disabilities has resulted in the necessity of finding viable ways of providing for them. Educational programs, many of which claim to be a cure-all, are being developed in large numbers. Many professionals in special and general education suggest that the present system is actually *creating* learning-disabled students and that, once labeled, these students learn how to be helpless since the approaches used in teaching emphasize their weaknesses. When approaches and programs are developed with the notion of overcoming a learning disability, they often fail to meet the unique style of the individual and since a person with a learning disability is often not a flexible learner, she becomes *more* confused by the approach. Actual experiences of individuals with learning disabilities suggest that we should be doing just the opposite and help them develop and use their strengths as well as their coping skills. Dayle speaks with insight and years of personal experience when she says, "A learning disability does not go away, one simply learns to work around it, to use the strategies presented by teachers and to accept the disability as an impediment but never a barrier to making one's dreams come true."

Each chapter in *Making the Grade* includes a reflection on being learning disabled and a commentary on that reflection. A list of the coping strategies that were mentioned in the reflection and commentary appears at the end of each chapter. Appendix A includes an alphabetized compilation of all the strategies, with suggestions for their use with students. Appendix B provides an annotated list of books, journals, organizations, and materials that others have found useful in understanding and educating individuals with learning disabilities.

1

Early Childhood

Putting Order in My Life

REFLECTION

Let's begin. I come from a well-educated family. There are individuals with doctorates on both sides of my family. My mother is a registered nurse and my father has a master's degree in agronomy. Both of my parents love to read just for the joy of it. This is something I still find hard to believe because I found only pain in reading. Their continued involvement in their respective fields even though they are both retired is commendable and proof to me that learning is, indeed, a life-long journey.

My mother had a normal pregnancy with me and reports no problems during that time or at birth. My progress from birth until fourteen months was normal, if not somewhat advanced in the motor and language development areas. I walked at eleven months of age and was stringing words together successfully. Soon after my first birthday, I developed a cold that turned into pneumonia. I had a temperature of 104 to 105 degrees for about four hours and was taken to the hospital, where I quickly recovered. About six months later, I had croup and from that time on have had bouts of bronchitis. Like many other children, I had mild cases of mumps and chicken pox. Now, I am sharing this for two reasons: One is that people looking for early correlates of learning disabilities will have information about my developmental background to consider; the second reason is that parents of children with learning disabilities can compare their children's early years with mine.

I rode a two-wheeler before I was four years old. I did scribble writing, made wonderful finger paintings, and stayed in the lines of coloring books before I started school. My language development, even after the early illnesses and fever, remained normal if not a little advanced, according to my parents who compared me to my older sister, who was later an excellent student.

I would listen for hours to someone who told me a story. My grandfather told the best stories. I can't remember if they were true or not, but I do remember that he often had a hard time recalling the ones I would ask him to retell. I would then tell the story back to him, almost word for word. Both of my parents remark on what a wonderful memory I always had, even from the earliest times. My mother would read to me; again, I could repeat most of the stories (long or short) word for word, anywhere she started in the story. Another thing I remember is that I loved to watch people doing things—anything. I would spend hours observing an activity, taking in every detail of an activity such as hanging up clothes. I knew which pieces were hung together, which separately, how far over their edges the towels were hung, how closely the edges of other items were hung, and where the clothespins were placed. I recall being upset when these activities weren't done exactly the same way each time. I would get confused. I noticed pictures that were hung crooked, checked people's collars that were turned up or over, socks or shoes that didn't match. I mostly remember how much it bothered me when things were out of place, as if somehow the picture didn't match the negative I had in my mind. I always felt I had to put things back where they should be so that I would not be so upset.

Once, when we lived in an old house, I went around and took all the door handles apart and showed them to my mother, expecting her to be as pleased with me as I was with myself. She tried for some time to put one back together with little success. She then asked me if I could put the locks back together, which I did with great speed. I had watched my father fix one once and found it fascinating. My mother announced that if I ever took them apart again, I would be in trouble. I didn't take the locks apart again! However, I would take apart everything else, and put it back together again. Toys, clocks, furniture, record players—all were duly disassembled and then correctly assembled again. Not satisfied with one such mechanical feat, I would do it over and over and over, never seeming to get bored. Once, my sister Diane and I got locked in the bathroom and Diane couldn't open the door, which had a bolt with different stops on it. Dad came to the other side of the door and tried to explain to Diane how the lock worked while I sat on the floor, listening and watching. After some time, with my sister getting nowhere with the directions, Dad asked me if I could open the door. I did so handily. When I was asked why I hadn't opened the door when I first understood Dad's directions, I responded that he had asked Diane to do it, not me!

I climbed trees and could catch and hit a ball, both physical skills that enabled me to play with the older kids. I thought that was great, though my older sister was not always pleased about the situation. I remember Diane taking dancing lessons. I was too young for the lessons, so I just watched the teacher. When we got home, Diane would try to do the steps, sometimes forgetting the instructions. Since I could see the teacher in my mind's eye, and could copy her steps, I was always able to show Diane the correct steps. Today, I can still see the room, the little wooden fold-up chairs, and my sister trying to do a pirouette.

I remember wondering about how the sky grew dark and if God had a big shade he pulled down and up again to make it light, wondered why it never got all tangled up like ours sometimes did if we overslept and pulled up the shade too fast. I wondered if my bike had bigger tires, would it go faster? Since the bike went faster than the trike, were the number of wheels the reason for the speed or was it because the bike had one less tire? Would cars go faster if they only had two tires? Why didn't my bike have an accelerator? It had brakes!

Sometimes I listened to my records on the record player, over and over and over. I listened maybe fifteen or twenty times in a row, or until the picture in my head was complete—for there always was a film playing in my head. After a while, the film was complete down to the very last detail. Let me explain. When I played the record "Davy Crockett," I first listened and imagined a picture of what I thought Davy Crockett looked like, moved like, and sounded like. Having satisfactorily stored that information, I went on to the phrase "king of the wild frontier." I asked my mother what this king would look like, then made a picture in my head of that and how Davy fit into it. Next came the phrase "born on a mountain top in Tennessee." This was the hard part—I had to rearrange the picture so this scene could come before Davy was a "king." I had to imagine mountains, then put a house on top. I had to decide what the house looked like outside and inside, what Davy looked like as a baby, what his parents looked like, and so forth. My mother would tell me that I seemed to be lost in space when I really was lost in the complex making of my film, assuring that all the pieces were in the right place.

My three favorite records were "Davy Crockett," "Daniel Boone," and "The Teddy Bears' Picnic." I made films of all the records in my head, and would be very upset if someone showed me a picture book of the stories and the pictures or sequence in the book didn't match the picture in my head.

COMMENTARY

In this chapter, Dayle reflects upon her early life and some of her experiences during those early developmental stages. This is important, both for what it says about the normalcy of a child who will later be diagnosed as learning disabled, and for what Dayle remembers as strengths that as a student she eventually turned into strategies basic to success in school.

Often when we look for precedents to a learning disability, we expect to find a basis for the later problem in early childhood. School records are filled with suspected early correlates of the disability, such as slow or faulty language development, poor large and/or small motor coordination, and hyperactivity. Dayle had none of these characteristics. As a matter of fact, her parents believed that her language and motor development were advanced during her preschool years.

Learning disabilities are often attributed to prenatal problems, poor nutrition, illness resulting in high fevers, and perhaps even hospitalization, which can interfere with bonding and language recognition development. Dayle did have a number of childhood illnesses, specifically, pneumonia resulting in high temperatures and recurring bronchitis. But there was no noticeable result of the illnesses, as her parents reported no change in any area of her preschool development. As for other suspected correlates, such as poor nutrition, lack of family interest in education, few middle-class experiences, and little emphasis on reading, none of this applies to Dayle's early life. It is clear that Dayle's parents were well educated and, according to her memory, were very interested in their children's activities. She was surrounded by people who read to her, told imaginative stories, and were avid readers themselves.

Although few of the negative correlates of learning disabilities were evident in Dayle's preschool years, her strengths were already beginning to show. Her memory was excellent: She recalled even the minutest details of stories she heard or books that were read to her. She seemed especially skilled at visualizing what she heard (such as the lock in the bathroom) and remembering in enough detail what she saw to repair toys, clocks, and furniture. Although she was not efficient later at using visual memory as a helpful strategy for beginning reading or writing, she was unusually skilled at remembering stories, pictures, and objects that had meaning for her.

Another of Dayle's strengths that emerged early was her ability to organize the objects in her world. This, along with her memory, allowed her to make films in her mind based on stories she had heard. As we will discover, this strategy became very important in her later schooling as she converted lectures and discussions into visual images and stories.

This organizational ability of Dayle's actually came close to being a weakness when it became a compulsion for her to put things into place. She grew upset when she saw paintings and photographs hung askew, collars turned wrong, and so forth. There were times later in her life when her need for order in the scene around her caused her a great deal of anxiety. It is quite possible that this need to organize her environment became a way for Dayle to control objects around her, since she later found that school presented much that she could not control. In other words, she repeated the tasks she could do well over and over, because she failed so often at those academic tasks that her classmates could perform well.

Tied in with Dayle's need for organization is a rule-following behavior that sometimes makes her appear quite naive. For Dayle, certain rules underlie correct organization. Not only must those rules be followed when folding and hanging towels, but also when making moral decisions. If it's wrong to steal apples from the trees in an apple orchard, it is also wrong to pick up fallen rotting apples from the ground. There are no gray areas; decisions are either black or white.

Another early-emerging strength that has helped Dayle considerably over the years is persistence. When Dayle is determined, she will do any task again and again until she is successful. Without that characteristic and without the people who have helped guide her toward a correct finished product, Dayle would never have been able to accomplish what she has academically.

2

Elementary School

Learning I Am Different

REFLECTION

I want to share so many issues from this period in my life, it's difficult to know where to start.

> Why am I all dressed up? What is that great big place, and what are all those kids doing here? School? Mom, where are you going? You didn't say anything about leaving me here alone. I don't know any of these kids, I don't like the smell of this place, and I don't know who that person is who is smiling at me. Oh, a teacher, sure, I know what teachers do. Big enough to stay alone, sure, I can do that. I am a big girl. Cry? Never! Pick me up when they let me out. Are they going to lock me in or something? Oh, I see, okay, you'll be right here. You won't be late, will you?

I knew I was different from my classmates around the second week of school. The other children seemed to understand what this school system was all about. They seemed to know why and when we were to go somewhere or to begin to work on a specific task. How did they know these things? While I was trying to figure out how they knew, I needed to find some way to stay out of trouble. So I chose the children who always seemed to be in the teacher's good graces and decided to do exactly what they did. When they picked up their chairs to form a circle, I did the same. When they began to read silently, I too, read silently. When they lined up to go someplace, I followed. This seemed to work. Then, there was the question of time. I knew what time school started, when we had morning recess, when lunch was, when we had afternoon recess, and when it was time to go home. To me, time was an event followed by another event. It would be years before I would actually understand the *concept* of time.

Reading was another interesting concept. Have you ever asked a child what he or she thought reading was? It's an interesting project and one worth investigating. For myself, reading entailed repeating a story my mother told me about different books. Mom would tell some great stories, too. Little did I know she was reading the stories to me. It would be years before I understood that words were made up of individual squiggles (letters) whose individual sounds combined to make words. I would memorize the stories Mom read and repeat them to the teacher and students in school.

It wasn't until halfway through second grade that the teacher discovered I had little or no understanding of what reading really meant. Up until that time, I simply repeated what had been told to me. We were not given our reading books to take home over vacation and when we returned to school we were told to form our reading groups. We were given new books and I was chosen to start the first sentence. How was I going to tell a story I had never heard? The teacher was shocked. My parents were stunned. I didn't catch on to reading that year, so I repeated the second grade. I was caught in a tidal wave that would take forty-four years to swim out of and to survive. I am aware now that I spent the rest of my school life constructing a web of strategies strong enough for me to survive in an academic environment, one day at a time. (Based on my experiences, I feel the decision to have a child repeat a grade should be given careful consideration, and should be an option only when there are no others.)

During the summer after my second year, my mother bought the book, *Why Johnny Can't Read*. I couldn't understand what Johnny had to do with me. Johnny was a boy, and I was a girl. I was totally confused by the words in *Why Johnny Can't Read*. My mom gave me the words *was, want, what, which, went, where, why,* and *who* in sequence and I learned them. I could repeat them on command. But when my father changed the sequence, I couldn't "read" the words any more. He didn't understand my problem, and he lost patience. He asked, "How could you come up with *saw* when all the words begin with *w*?" The summer continued . . . *what, who, when . . .*

Third grade was a wonderful year. We had moved. I was going to attend a new school and I thought this would be a new start when I would finally learn to read, write, and spell. I was already using cursive to write. This would be something I could help the other students learn. Miss Besser was tall, older, smelled like spring flowers, and wore brightly colored, weird clothes. She asked me if I could write her name on the board. Pleased to be asked, I strutted to the blackboard and wrote "Miss Besser." All the students started to laugh. I knew right then that there was something about me that told the other kids I was stupid. Was it something about the way I dressed? Maybe something about my body? My eyes were too close together or too wide apart? Maybe it was the way I stood, or my feet were funny looking? There must have been something about me that stood out like a neon sign flashing, "This kid is stupid, stupid. . . ."

Miss Besser dismissed the class for recess and asked me to stay. She asked me if I saw anything wrong with what I had written. No, I had formed all the letters just right, and I was sure I had even spelled her name correctly. She then picked up the chalk and wrote her name over what I had written on the board. I was shocked. The other kids must have thought I was some kind of freak. I knew that I would never again be able to look them in the eye. What was I thinking? How could I do something so dumb? I started to cry. I was finished as a child, student, person. I was sure I would never be able to hold my head up as long as I lived. Miss Besser hugged me and told me we would work on this problem together. We would take one step at a time. She thought I was smart. She thought I had lots of strengths. She thought I could do all these school things. She thought it may take some extra time, and we may have to go slowly, but she had no doubt I could do whatever I set out to accomplish. Looking back, I think we worked on self-esteem issues that year more than we worked on academic issues.

Because I had stayed back a grade, I was bigger and taller than the other students in my class. That year, I decided to take matters into my own hands when it came to disciplining the other students. I no longer would tell the teacher which students were teasing or picking on me because I had trouble reading; now, I would wait until those kids were on the playground and I would beat them up until a teacher separated us. I did spend a lot of time in the vice principal's office! We had conversations about what was right and wrong, and ways to deal with anger. I wondered why all the teachers and the vice principal were talking to me. I would not have had to act this way if the kids hadn't teased me. Why was I the one who had to change?

One day, our neighbor's daughter was taking things out of our garage. I had told her never to touch my bat, ball, or glove. I looked out the window and there she was—with all three. I ran out of the house and tackled her. I began hitting her until I saw red. The next thing I remember was that my dad had me under his arm and I was still swinging. Looking down, I saw the girl was bleeding and not getting up. Dad put me down and took care of the girl. When he got back to me, he asked what had happened. I explained. We had a long conversation. It ended with Dad telling me I was never again, as long as I lived, ever to hit another person because I could seriously injure the person. To this day, I have never raised a hand to anyone in anger.

My fifth-grade teacher was lots of fun. He had wires strung high on all four walls around his classroom. Each wall represented a subject: math, science, history, and English. As he talked about a specific topic he hung a 6 × 10 card over the wire. The card had a picture of the event or topic with two or three sentences about the picture. For example, for the topic the Civil War, the person was Abraham Lincoln, and the event was the Battle of Gettysburg. He hung these cards in order and asked us review questions based on the cards. When he gave us a quiz or test, he took the cards down. I always got to put the cards back because I could remember the sequence better than all the other students. I also got good (not great) grades because I could recall the picture and the story that went with the picture. I could do this for all four subjects.

When I was in fifth grade, my younger sister, Debra, was born. I thought my parents had her just for me. Debra was mine to take care of, to teach, and to love. Little did I know, she would end up helping me read, write, and spell during my high school years as she continues to do even today.

During my sixth-grade year, we did a lot of crafts. We made presents for gifts. Those gifts involved math, writing, research, group, and individual work. I thought we were getting away with something since I never expected a teacher to be sneaky enough to make school work fun. We made paper maché continents. I still can picture Africa in my mind's eye and think of all the different topics covered in that one activity. We did mapmaking, math (it had to be done to scale), history, geography, writing, science, and so forth—and all the time I thought we were playing. Ah, this was the way school should be. As I got older, I realized what had happened in this class. Since then, I have wondered why all of school could not be like this. The way I respond to situations, my emotional well-being, and how I relate to students is the result of those elementary school years. How we were treated has a direct bearing on how we treat ourselves and others years later. I feel that it's ironic that I, once a special education student, am now teaching children with special needs. Words hurt me, no matter where I was, in the classroom or on the playground. As parents and educators, we need to remember the power of both the written and spoken word to harm and inspire.

COMMENTARY

Dayle knew in the first grade that she was not like the other students in her class. They learned that written symbols and reading were connected, they learned how to read the clock correctly. Dayle did not understand the connections between written and oral symbols. Individuals with learning disabilities tend to be very concrete in their thinking and learning, and have trouble with abstract concepts. What could be more abstract than written squiggles that apparently stand for spoken sounds, and, when combined in certain ways, actually represent meaning? Most of us learn easily that the symbol *b* has a corresponding sound and that several such sounds combine to make a word. For some people, these connections are not easily made since the written symbol *b* has no inherent meaning, nor does the sound say *buh*. Even when a poor reader is able to memorize the symbols, the writing (grapheme) and the sounds (phonemes) are not consistent. (If the word *could* begins with a *c*, then what does *city* begin with?) Learning the phonics rules does not help either, because they are also abstract. (Why should *c* before *o* be a hard *c*, whereas *c* before *i* is soft? And what are "hard" and "soft" sounds, anyway?)

Telling time is as abstract as learning to read, and many children with learning disabilities find the concept difficult (Lerner, 1993; Trumbull, 1976). When we consider that time on a clock merely represents the passage of activities somewhere else (certainly not on the face of the clock), we begin to realize how abstract this clock-reading skill actually is!

Early in her schooling, Dayle began to develop her own coping strategies. She learned to read body language so she could figure out what postures were taken by teachers and students when certain activities were to take place. She found that telling time was very difficult, but she memorized the configuration of the hands when certain events happened. As she grew up, Dayle began to develop for herself some strategies using her strengths of visualization, listening, memory, and communication. She had (and still has) an overwhelming fear of being "discovered" and being put in a position where she will have to reveal her poor reading and writing skills. Thus, she began early to develop strategies such as reading ahead of time everything she might be asked to read in class, identifying people who would edit her writing and who could explain to her verbally certain directions so she could use her visual strengths to create a "map" in her mind.

Typical of those with learning disabilities, Dayle became more and more certain that she was less intelligent than her classmates as she progressed through her school years. As we have seen, reading and writing were the most difficult academic skills for her to master. Since those abilities seemed to underlie everything she did academically, she began to believe that she was incompetent at everything. She found that she could not simply overcome these disabilities through remediation; instead, she had to develop strategies for coping with them.

As she recounts her school-age frustrations with reading books, Dayle admits to substituting words she could not read with others that fit the content. This strategy works for many students with learning disabilities; in fact, it should be encouraged. Sometimes Dayle is unable to match the phonemes (sounds) making up the word to the graphemes (letters) she sees on the page. Or she may be able to match the phoneme with the grapheme, but she cannot actually read the word, because it is not in her vocabulary. (People who do not read much usually have smaller vocabularies than those who read a lot.) Since Dayle has trouble sounding out words, her pronunciation of new names and places can differ dramatically from the correct pronunciation, thus adding to her frustration about discussing what she has read in class. Again, she has learned to engage others in conversation about the reading so she can hear how words are pronounced.

See Appendix A for strategies in generalizing, reading, spelling, and time telling.

3

Junior High School
Disappointment and Discovery

REFLECTION

SEVENTH GRADE

What a wonderful place junior high is going to be! I'm going to change classes, have different teachers, and see different students. I'm going to make a bunch of new friends and I'm going to be a great student. This is going to be the best year I've ever had in school. The teachers will not know my background, so I will have a whole new chance of making school turn out all right. I'm going to ride the bus with my sister and go to games, dances, and plays with her. This is going to be the greatest. All that testing will tell them that I am O.K. and they will give me another chance. They have to, because I'm going to this new school where no one knows me or my history.

It's the first day of school and I can hardly wait until I get to my homeroom, where there are new kids for me to meet! I'll get lots of books and a locker, and I'll get to walk around the school, going from one class to the next. This is what I have waited for all my life. I think about all this on the bus ride to school. I have pictures of this day drifting by in my mind's eye and what a glorious day it's going to be. Everyone likes me and I can do all the work they ask me to do. I'll get *As* on all my work and the teachers will post it all over the school. What a day! The air is crisp and smells clean, the sky is deep blue, and the trees are just starting to have a hint of color to them. Life is wonderful and all is right with the world!

The walk from the bus up the sidewalk to that beautiful, old building is a pleasure. I have on nice, new clothes, the wait is almost over and I am a junior-high student at long last. Even the doors are great—large, wooden, and brown, with just the right touch of brass. Up the old marble staircase I run; to my homeroom, to my desk, and to my teacher.

Looking around the room in blissful happiness, I suddenly get a strange feeling. I have never seen so many kids with different handicaps. But, what the heck, maybe this is the year they've all gotten into the public school system. While on my incredible high, the teacher begins to talk and I listen. Something is terribly wrong. What she is saying does not match the picture in my mind. I'm having trouble understanding what she is saying and why she is saying it. This is going to be our classroom, we are going to have a wonderful and productive year. Well, obviously, I must be in the wrong room, that's all. I'll just tell the teacher that there must be some mistake and she'll send me to the right classroom. Everything is going to be OK.

> What do you mean, I'm in the right room? There must be some mistake, can you check with someone else? No, I'm not being fresh, I just don't want to be in this classroom. I am supposed to be in a class that moves from room to room. I'm supposed to have a clean slate, you're not supposed to know anything about me. I'm not dumb and you can't do this to me! I have to get out of here.

As I leave the room, the teacher follows me and tries to explain to me that I will only be in this classroom until I can prove that I can do the work, and until the test results come back, but until then, I must stay in this class. All those chances gone, all the new clothes for nothing, all my new friends gone. My life comes to a dead stop. There is no motion. I go back to my desk in a void. Looking around the class, I hate these students. All the dumb kids are in one class now, in the corner classroom out of the way of the fast, smart kids. My heart pounds as I return to my black, safe world, where I stay for about two weeks, hating my parents, family, and friends, but mostly that dark, ugly building with the big, jail doors and the worn, dirty stairs with my classroom in the corner, hidden from the real, the good, the smart students.

TWO WEEKS LATER

This is great, and I am the smartest kid in the class. I even get to help the other students with their work. I like being smart; yes, this is nice. I get to run errands, deliver notes, and correct papers. I wonder why they won't let us go from class to class. I wonder what is wrong with all the kids in my class? We all seem to go at our own speed and we are having a good time with the work and we help each other a lot. I wonder if that is wrong. I wonder if school is supposed to be an unhappy place. I wonder if I just don't get what school is all about. I wonder what will happen to my friends in this class, and when they will be able to get out of here and go from class to class like the good kids. I wonder if *we* are good kids. Maybe we are bad! I know that sometimes we do bad things. I guess maybe we are bad and dumb. I guess that is why we are here; because we are both!

Well, too bad for the rest of the world, because we are having a ball. We help each other and most of the time we have fun. We even get to fix our mistakes. I get to put marks in the teacher's rank book and to figure out what our grades are. Sometimes I give everyone just a few more points (only two or three—well, sometimes five if it was a really hard assignment) to help us out a little. We don't get to see the other students much because we do most things by ourselves. Art, music, and phys. ed. are some of the classes we do all by ourselves. The best part is that we get to eat alone, and the staff is nice. They serve us extra food. I think they feel sorry for us but they don't need to, because we are just fine. Some of the kids like to make the staff feel that way because it makes some of us feel good—like being "one up" on everyone else.

Life continued like this until just before Thanksgiving. All my test results had come back. The uncomfortable feeling was back. Things were about to change. I wondered how the results could make things worse. All I really knew for sure was that something was about to happen.

The test results said that I had a high average IQ, with lots of peaks and valleys. But since my peaks were higher than my valleys were low, this was interpreted to mean that I wasn't trying as hard as I should. However, everyone agreed that I had some kind of language problem, and they used the word "dyslexia," whatever that meant. So in the wisdom of the testing establishment, I became an average student and put immediately into a different classroom where all the students were doing everything I thought I wanted to do. Except I never got to say good-bye to my old classmates, never got to visit, and never again had that sense of happiness that I could get to the top in my class or even be considered a good student. Students always referred to me as the kid who came from the dummy class. I was both angry and excited, happy and sad. Looking back, this is where I believe counseling for me should have started. I needed to deal with all those feelings one at a time and put closure on that period of my life. Instead, that whole year, I played catch-up. I had missed all of the review I needed so badly during the months of September and October. The students were already studying new material that I never really grasped. It was a long year, and the thrill of changing classes, meeting new friends, and seeing the big wooden doors with the touch of brass in the same magical light, was forever tarnished.

EIGHTH GRADE

This is going to be a new year, in a new state, in a new school, and I hope I'll make some new friends. The teachers probably know I am not the best student in the world. I don't know how they know, but they always do. I'll have a tour of the school tomorrow. When we were out shopping, Dad drove around the school so I could see what it looks like. There is a brand new building, the gym; boy, it looks huge.

The big day has come! I'm glad it's summer and there are few people around. As we walk down the sidewalk, my heart pounds, and I feel a little dizzy. We walk into the office where the principal greets us. He's bald, and shorter than my dad (Dad is very tall, so that's not unusual), but I expect principals to be tall. He seems very nice, but it's like I am not here, he only talks to my parents. I wonder why he is talking to them, when I am the one who will be going to school here. He walks us around the school. It looks to me like every other school, and smells like all schools do. We go into the home economics room. I think: *What a waste of time this is, all those ovens, I can't believe I have to take a class in here, what a bore.* A woman walks in and is she tall, taller than the principal (she must have lots of power) and she smells like something good to eat. This may not be so bad; I like her already. The only place I really want to see is the gym. When we get there it's the greatest, with all the latest equipment. I think that three of my old gyms could fit in this one. I think it's the most wonderful place I have ever seen! I forget about everything else and focus on this one place. Little do I know that this large room will be my savior during the next five years, the place that will let me shine, even if only for a short time. I even get to meet the physical education teacher; she has dimples (I don't know anyone with dimples) and she seems very nice. On the ride home, I walk the halls and meet the teachers again in my mind's eye. Over and over, I play the tape, until it's printed in a groove somewhere deep in my brain. This gives me great comfort. All those things I wished for last year are here in this place. But I am afraid tomorrow all the good feelings will be gone, and I am not going to take any chances. The hurt is too great and I can't deal with it just now. I need to concentrate on getting through a day. I need to be safe, make sure the next step will not set me up for failure and humiliation.

Sometime during the first weeks, I find myself in social studies class and in the middle of "reviewing the world." For years I have spent my school days keeping everything separate in my mind. For example, there is reading in English, reading in science, reading in math, and reading in social studies. I always thought they were very different and had nothing in common because the vocabulary was so different. I never thought of reading as a whole category. Everything in my mind was in its own file, in no particular order. Now, here in social studies class, the teacher is using an overhead. She puts a map of the world on the machine. She then overlays the world map with a map of the United States. *You can't do that,* I think, *it won't work.* In my mind I have very separate maps, one of Exeter, my town, one of New Hampshire, one of the United States, and one of the world. One does not have anything to do with another. When the teacher points to the map of the world and asks me to tell her about my state, I think she is joking, because she has never discussed that state. However, when she points to a single map of New Hampshire, I tell her about its geology, its history, its people; I give her far more information than she wants! The teacher considers this to be fresh; she keeps me after school to learn good manners.

I had never learned to generalize. Instead, I had spent my life making sure everything was kept pure and clear of clutter, for fear that I might not be able to find the information I needed. For the first time in my life, I wondered if everything was like that. Was an inch on a ruler the same as an inch on a yard stick and an inch on a tape measure? Was there only one kind of reading? I have a great deal of admiration for my poor mother, who answered all these questions without getting upset. I spent the rest of the year emptying my small files and making connections, generalizing, categorizing, and organizing new files. These concepts were new to me and I found that many things were interrelated. It was a wonderful discovery. Every day, more links were made. I was so tired at the end of each day! I remember being tired all that year; my mind seemed to be empty in some areas and be overloaded in others. This was also the year that I became aware of social skills—why people liked some people but not others. Until this time I was totally concerned with survival and reading body language, voice tones, any little nuance that might indicate I was in trouble. I never related to how people made and kept friends. Considering all this, eighth grade and third grade were both the biggest (I discovered skills) and smallest (I'd discovered my weaknesses) growth periods in my life. I call this year "the year of nesting," in which everything seemed to fit together and intertwine with something else.

COMMENTARY

Dayle's first year of junior high—the seventh grade—had an effect on her that she was never able to fully overcome. Dayle was a failure again, and now she was convinced that she was "dumb." If a teacher or counselor had told her about her new placement at the junior high, she didn't hear or fully understand that she was going to be in the class with the low-functioning students. It didn't matter that the new testing proved that she was not retarded, she could not do the work required of her in the classroom. Her parents knew that Dayle had many skills and that she never forgot anything that she learned but they couldn't understand why she was having so much trouble learning. Her dad began to tell her that she needed to try harder.

Although Dayle had the *intelligence* to succeed in the regular classroom, she did not have the *skills* necessary to do the work required of her. After all, academic success is based on reading and writing. As Dayle points out in her reflection, the first month or so of school was a review of the work from the previous year so that all the students who had arrived from different elementary schools could become accustomed to their new setting and the teachers could get to know the students and help them make the transition. Dayle missed this whole process, and for an individual who needed the transitional period desperately, she was at such a great disadvantage that she had no way to overcome it. The teachers, who were well on their way to the delivery of new information, were unable to support her appropriately because they did not know what to do. There were only the test results, which indicated Dayle could do the required school work; but in reality, she was unable to keep up with her classmates. Her dad and teachers, not knowing what else to say, asked her to try harder and when she did, with no success, they labeled her lazy. As a group, teachers today know more about the facts of learning disabilities. However, few of them know how to help such a student in the regular classroom. When Dayle was at this level, very few teachers even recognized the term *learning disability.*

Dayle's negative experiences in the seventh grade clearly resulted in an emotional component to the learning disability. Although federal law defines a learning disability as not being the result of an emotional disturbance (U.S. Office of Education, 1968), emotional problems can—and do—arise as the result of a learning disability, which clearly interferes with a major part of the school curriculum. An intelligent person who, try as she might, cannot meet the criteria essential to success in the academic culture will certainly suffer the emotional consequences of that failure. At that point in her school career, Dayle certainly needed counseling from both an understanding teacher and a trained school counselor. Those seventh-grade experiences only supported her failures in elementary school. Her self-esteem, which had improved with the knowledge that she was entering a new school, plummeted. She had many strong skills that some of her teachers may have recognized, yet those skills were not capitalized on, and her failures became the focus.

Although Dayle's family moved again before she entered the eighth grade, she had no illusions about her success this year. The previous year had left her with too much hurt to expect that she could start again with a clean slate. This year, Dayle pinned her hopes on sports, and the gym became the only bright spot in school. The excitement of being in a new school quickly faded. Dayle realized that she could never attain academic success. Perhaps, if she turned her attention to sports, she could gain some credibility.

Dayle had a worthwhile experience at the beginning of the year when she discovered in social studies that she could actually make connections among some of the skills she was learning. Her concrete way of thinking had prevented her from understanding that a skill she learned in one context was still the same skill when placed in another context. Reading was reading, whatever class she was in; measuring provided the same results whether she used a ruler or a yardstick; fractions worked in science class the same way they worked in math; and Exeter was still Exeter, whether it was described as a part of New Hampshire or a town in the United States. She was learning how to generalize, a skill most children begin to develop in early childhood. Because of their very concrete thinking styles, many individuals with learning disabilities have trouble seeing similarities and thus categorizing; an apple and an orange are both fruits, a more useful description than, "you can eat them both, and they are both round." The concept of *fruit* is abstract, whereas eating and shape are very concrete. In making that conceptual leap, Dayle was able to solve problems more easily than she had before. Now, instead of creating an entirely new solution for each problem, she could categorize objects and then generalize common information to new situations in which many of the attributes were similar. Generalizing is not intuitive, it is learned; but it's not an easy learning process for someone with a learning disability.

See Appendix A for strategies in anticipation, categorization, counseling, generalization, inclusion, and organization.

4

High School
Becoming an Expert at Deception

REFLECTION

I look back now and wonder how I made it to my high school graduation. I am surprised I wasn't thrown out. Now, as a teacher of students with learning disabilities, I witness students who act like I did or who say similar things. I showed little respect for adults. I constantly "tested" them, and only a few passed. These special few seemed too good to be true.

In ninth grade, I finally decided to hand in my homework. Homework was something I never had enough time for. But it seemed I acquired much knowledge during the summer between the eighth and ninth grades. I pretended to be much more confident. It seemed I had become much smarter, and I wondered how everyone else had become somewhat inferior. With my newly gained confidence, I decided to do my homework. My solution was to do English on Mondays, math on Tuesdays, science on Wednesdays, social studies on Thursdays, and give myself Fridays off. To me, this would take care of the time crunch I always felt and I could actually pass in assignments. But I gave up doing my homework about three weeks later when I found that my plan was not exactly approved by the teachers, who wanted the homework done on a daily basis. Work not done had to be made up and future work had to be handed in on time. By this time I was feeling very creative. The teachers' solution was for me to stay after school every afternoon until the backlog of work was done to their satisfaction. My solution was simply not to do any more homework at all.

This sounds like an act of defiance, doesn't it? Well, let's look at this from my point of view. In class, I was rarely called upon to answer questions. The assumption, I think, was that if I did not do the homework, I probably was not prepared for class. I could, however, answer any question they would

23

ask me. They just didn't ask. There was nothing wrong with my hearing or my sight. I also liked the one-on-one attention I would get from the teacher after school. Negative attention is always better than no attention at all! Because the teachers did not expect anything from me, I believed that they thought I was not capable of doing the work required of me. Therefore, if they thought I was dumb, I would see to it that their perceptions were correct. I was, after all, so much wiser now.

My best friends were the brightest students in the class. They were in all the advanced classes and I only got to see them during lunch or physical education, art, or music classes. They excelled at everything academic. They were the stars, the most popular students, they could write and read their written words aloud, they shared their gifts with other students, and they were made to feel accepted and special. The girls were all in the same physical education class. We also were all on the field hockey team, and we all played intramural sports. My coping strategy for classes was to escape in my mind's eye to a safe, gentle place where I excelled. I was the star, I was popular, I could say and write the most powerful words, I was wise and could help the other students with their assignments and I would never make them feel or believe they were worthless. I became very popular, the afternoon student who could be of all sorts of help. When given permission and encouragement, I could do an excellent job of correcting papers, helping other students with problems, and the staff thought I was great.

I also had a dark side that would take over once in a while. For instance, I encouraged a very tall student to do handstands on the desk while I put ink on the bottom of his shoes so that he could leave footprints on the ceiling tiles. For our snow sculpture, I talked the class into making a very large (and well insulated) Frankenstein casket with an arm and hand folded like a Victory sign. Of course, it was the last bit of snow to melt in the spring. I convinced our class not to sing the school song during assemblies. None of the adults ever found out how all this was accomplished. My dad once asked if I had anything to do with these events and I would tell him that I did not participate in the event itself. His only answer was, "Yes, but who instigated these special little doings?" Thank God he never did wait for an answer.

I remember the time I had almost read a whole book, all but the last chapter. I felt as though I was doing the teacher a favor by reading so much. It also gave me a great deal of confidence. I delivered the report, ready for her questions. She didn't question me and as I sat down, I was sure that I had received the first solid *A* of my high school career. Finally, I received the grade; it was a solid *D*⁺! The teacher wrote:

> The book was not long enough, was not appropriate for this subject, and the listeners did not know how the book ended. However, the presentation was very good and that's why I gave you a passing grade.

Once again, I made the decision: I would never put myself through the hours and agony of trying to sift through all those words to please her. I had her for all four years of school. When I became a special education teacher, I often wondered why teachers who appeared less compassionate were those assigned to teach the less able or more challenging students. From that day on I did book reports in the following way. I made up a story as I was walking back and forth from home to school. When I finished assembling the report, I went to the library and picked out a publishing company and an author. Most of the time, I received a *B* or *C* on these reports. If the teacher assigned a specific book list, I asked my friends if they had read or written a book report on any of the books. Then, I would memorize what they had written and rewrite the story. I got good marks on those reports, too. When I was a senior, I often changed the story line as I told the story to the class just to make things a little more exciting. The teacher would often comment on the fact that she had never read any of these books and I would say that they were in the junior high reading section because they were easier to read and hoped that was all right. I got to be an expert on deception.

As the years progressed, my typical day existed in a safe, private world. During classes, I would listen and try to relate what the teacher was saying to all my other classes, figuring out if there were any connections. The files in my head were in constant use. When I was called on in class, I would just sit there, and if the teacher insisted on an answer from me, I became the class clown and would keep joking until the bell rang. I often received threats that I would have to stay after school. When I got tired of trying to figure out what the teacher was saying and make all the connections I knew were necessary, I would do what I called mental exercises and think about practice or the next game. I called up the "video" of the last game and put it in slow motion, analyzed each and every pass and moves being made by both teams. If I could anticipate errors, perhaps we could end up the victor. These videos were so real that even today, I can see with great detail portions of those games.

When it came time for tests, I would just barely pass them, mostly because I never had time to finish the exams. It took me so long to read them that I would only finish two-thirds of the work, and if it was an essay test the teachers would always take points off for grammar, spelling, and organization. This left little space for me to excel. I would write short sentences, use short words I could spell, and try my darndest to organize the answer. As a senior, I wrote short stories about some nutty thing I had been thinking about rather than trying to read and write everything. If teachers were going to mark me off for not trying, why try?

The worst year of my entire academic life was my sophomore year, when my guidance counselor decided I should be on a college track. After all, I came from an educated family and if I would just try harder I could make the grade. Well, the first dilemma was to find a foreign language I could use (pass would be more like it). Off I went to see the French teacher and as I walked through the door, she held her hand up and said if I was coming to see if I could be in her class, her advice was to check with the Spanish teacher. Without saying a word, I turned around and went to see the Spanish teacher, who asked me if I knew the parts of speech. I had to think about that because I was pretty sure what nouns and verbs were but I was a little fuzzy about them. Her words of wisdom were that I should return to the guidance counselor and rethink this language thing. After the counselor and I talked for a while, he came up with the solution. I could take Latin because much of it would be close to the English language and it might even help me in English class. I was thinking, *I hope it's not too close to English or this could be a long year.* Well, I walked into "Mrs. Latin's" room the first day of class. In retrospect, I knew that I should have turned around and walked back out that very minute. But being my determined self, I went on in and began the year from hell.

English, Latin, biology, algebra, and the specials. I can honestly say I hated each and every class. I did not like the students, the classes, or the teachers. I walked around in a daze from the first to the last day of school. Even in these college-bound classes, I remained at the bottom of the heap. For example, if there were three biology classes, I was placed in the slowest class and I was one of the slowest students in that class. But at lunch I would help the students in the other biology classes with their homework, papers, and join in their decisions.

Mrs. Latin was a hundred-year-old woman who wore long, dark housedresses and thick, black, tie shoes. She had a round face with wire-rimmed glasses, wore her gray hair in a bun and often stood with her hands behind her back as she shared her wealth of knowledge. She did this with an unsmiling face, monotonous voice, lecture after lecture, every day for a year.

She was like the language itself: old, uninspiring, and predictably boring. I thought it my duty to add a little spice to her life and to the class. Her husband sent her a different colored rose every day, and at least once a week, I would do something like add a toy beetle or worm to a petal. I tried to answer all her questions and, of course, everyone would laugh. During the final exam, we were to translate a Latin passage. I leaned over to a fellow student and asked the title and how long the translation should be when finished. My classmate said, "four pages." I then wrote the title and proceeded to write a four-page story I invented about Rome and the gladiators. The following week, Mrs. Latin returned our exams and, standing with hands clasped behind her back, she announced, "For those of you who have two grades, the first one is for your imagination and the second is your grade." I had an *A/F!*

This was the year I learned some very important life skills. Washing blackboards became my specialty. My teachers had gotten together and decided I was having far too much fun after school. They decided I should wash all their blackboards every afternoon, and do at least some of the work required in the class as well as my homework. Little did they know that I liked the chore. I found it a challenge not to leave streaks and to do all four of them in less than twenty minutes. This, of course, included the prep and clean-up time. Teachers don't like to stay after school day after day, week after week, but I loved it. I thought I could win this game. Now there was only one major problem: Mrs. Latin. She would always keep me after school the day before a field hockey game, knowing that if I missed that practice I could not play in the game the next day. I was one of the best players on the team and I could encourage my teammates to perform amazing feats. I was worth a lot to the team! When I had to stay after school, the coach and some of my best friends held a later practice so I would be allowed to play on game days. It meant that the days were long but it was well worth the effort. I stayed in school.

At the end of a week that was particularly bad for me academically, my grades were in a downhill spiral and I wondered if I would ever be able to graduate. It was a beautiful spring day and we were playing softball against a new team. I was pitching and we were ahead thirty-three to nothing. I can't tell you how excited and powerful I felt. I was striking people out right and left, and I had a no-hitter going. My coach, the physical education teacher, took her starting team out at the beginning of the sixth inning and put in all the second string kids. I went absolutely nuts, screaming. She took me to the locker room, where she put me in the showers and told me to stay in the locker room until she came back. This woman was wonderful. Rather than give me a lecture on sportsmanship, she asked me what was bothering me. I replied angrily, "Why is it that every time I'm feeling good about myself and the team, I can't finish the game? But if I'm in class and failing, no one ever saves me. No one ever stops the great readers, spellers, and math whizzes, to let the second-string students play. When do I get to win?" She patted me on the back and said, "That's just one of the many things in life that aren't fair." My solution for myself was that no matter whether we had just finished a game, practice, or had a free day, I would go to the field and run until every muscle in my body burned, and then I would run around the field one more time. I ran to overcome my hurt and deal with my anger. My coach was always at the end of my run, and would walk back to the locker room with me in silence, sharing more than we ever could with voices. We never spoke of this again but to this day I know she understood more than anyone else ever would during those dark, black years.

Of course, I had the typical teenage experiences, too. Once, after we won a basketball game, we all threw each other into the showers and then had to go home with wet underwear. I had to walk home, and by the time I got there my underpants were frozen! Another time, I was invited to a dance and when my date and I got there, he sat with the boys on one side and I sat with the girls on the other, only meeting in the middle when the music started. I remember trying to cover up zits on my face with my mother's makeup, which of course only made them stand out more. Like many young girls, I sometimes wore a slip that was too long and had to roll it up around my waist to make it shorter. I loved to trade my lunch with other students for an ice cream sandwich or a piece of cake and thought it was hysterical to go to the movies with fourteen of us in the car. Now and then, my friends and I had such a great time in the public library that some of us were thrown out. I was never caught, but Dad was right to think I had a small hand in the making of the trouble.

It wasn't until my senior year that I began to think of the future and what I would do with the rest of my life. I had never given much thought to the fact that school would end. Just what was I going to do? My writing and reading skills were so low that I was sure job hunting would be even more humiliating than school. Most of my friends had gotten into the college of their choice, and were off to exciting futures. I was excited about this high school thing being over but terrified of what that meant. So, I decided to try and make amends for all my wrongdoing during these years. I began by being nice to the students who wanted to be on a team but were not athletic enough. Most of these kids had good grades, and I had always felt they were a little nervy trying out for a team. It would be like me trying to get in on the English debates. When I thought about this, I realized that they had more of a chance of reaching their goals than I would and I felt badly about the way I had treated them. So, my new goal was to help them succeed—or at least give it their best shot. I also decided that I should give homework one more try, at least for the teachers who were still giving me a chance. I turned in to the nicest person in the school. I began to give my most treasured belongings away and I tried desperately not to give the teachers a hard time. I became the model student. Sometime in February, my home economics teacher asked me to see her after school. When I went to see her, she was so serious that I thought she was about to tell me I would not be graduating with my class because of my grades. Instead, she asked if I was thinking about suicide. I was so shocked that she had so bluntly asked me, that I said, "Yes." I explained to her that everyone in my family was a success, my friends were successful, and that the only thing I excelled at was sports and that would come to an end when school was over. I had no other strengths, I told her, and I could not look to a future filled with the same pain I was feeling now. I had gone to several job interviews and had to fill out applications that I could not read. I couldn't even spell my place of birth, didn't know the difference between county and country when I read the two words, and I just could not handle the humiliation or pain much longer. I couldn't even open a checking account because I couldn't fill out the checks. I could never write out the amount of the check because I could not spell the numbers. I even told her about reading menus, how I hated chicken but it was the only word I was sure of and so that's what I ate at restaurants. I have never cried so long or hard in my life. I had reached the bottom and was drowning in my own tears.

After a long while, this wise and caring teacher explained these were not problems so large that we could not tackle them one at a time, and by graduation we could have plans in place that I would successfully handle most of the issues. As a beginning strategy, I was to collect as many job applications as I could. I asked my friends to help me find jobs they thought I could do well, and, with their help, had lots of applications by the following week. My teacher and I went through them and found all the common questions. On one side of a 3 × 5 card, I would write the answers to all these questions, and on the other side of the card, I would write words I had to use but could not spell. This way, I would have the correct spellings when I filled in the application. For the checking account, I took a 3 × 5 card and wrote the words *one* through *ten, eleven* through *twenty,* all the way to *one hundred.* This way, I had all the words I needed to write out the amounts of most checks. I needed other strategies to fill in the name of a store, and so forth. This could be done in several different ways. I could write down the names of the stores from advertising or from the signs outside the store. Then I could either keep the card handy or memorize the spelling of the most common stores. I have always kept one of those yellow sticky notes on the inside of my checkbook for this purpose. If I found myself in a store I did not know, I checked to find the name of the store and its spelling on store bags, at the counter, on the sales slip, or on in-store signs.

COMMENTARY

If Dayle had not been an excellent athlete, she might have given up in high school. As it was, she did come close to quitting—but the satisfaction she got from sports, along with her determination to keep playing, kept her in school. She is a perfect example of a student with learning disabilities who excels in a nonacademic activity but constantly lives with the threat of losing her place on the team if her grades drop. Other students suffer the same plight with art, music, and theater. Most curriculum rules dictate that traditional academics get primary attention, while the other subjects are secondary.

Most of the strategies Dayle used in high school were those that amused the other students and helped maintain her popularity among the friends with whom she could not compete academically. Her humor distracted teachers and often saved her from further embarrassment in class. Thus she used her leadership qualities, her sense of humor, and her skills in athletics as strategies to attain a certain measure of success. When she finally faced the fact that these strategies were not going to enable her to obtain any but the most menial job and that she certainly would not be able to go to college as all her friends would, she hit bottom. This happens to just about everyone who has a language-based disability. It's a turning point—either to despair or, as in Dayle's case, the beginning of an uphill battle into respectability as she defined it. In our culture, the ability to read and write is a necessity, not only for academic success but for financial success. Certainly, self-esteem suffers if a person fails at these basic skills.

Dayle's support system consisted of friends who cared about her and a special teacher who suggested strategies that would help her find a job after graduation. These were essential to Dayle's ability to go on with her life. A supportive family, sense of humor, and sheer determination to "make something" of herself were other factors, without which she would not have been able to overcome the reading and writing difficulties that prevented her from becoming successful in school.

Several of the strategies suggested in this reflection are addressed in the final paragraph, where her home economics teacher suggested them as ways to approach employment after graduation from high school. These and other strategies for book reports, homework, checking accounts, job applications, and support system, all useful for adolescents, are described in Appendix A.

5

Employment
Protecting Myself from the Inside

REFLECTION

I often think that I am different from other people with learning disabilities because I have always been employed. But the fact is that my early work history looks like that of a person who couldn't keep a job. My job history includes assembly-line worker, bank teller, accounting clerk, assistant head teller, supervisor in a data processing center, carpenter, and owner of a photography business.

I did a great job at all these places of employment. Ironically, I left because of promotions. I was afraid that I would not be able to do the reading or the writing that was required in a new position. So I would quit and look for a new job. I never thought to talk to my employers and tell them I liked what I was doing and wanted to continue in my present position. As I look back now, I realize that I didn't think I had any options other than to quit. It wasn't until a friend said something about my having a lot of jobs that I realized just how many places I had been employed.

I gave job hunting a great deal of thought. What was I going to do about this? What *could* I do about this? I was also dealing with anger and frustration. Counseling—that is what I could do. Off I went for counseling. But I found myself sitting in the counselor's office not saying anything. I went six times without saying a word, each time wondering where to start and realizing how much it cost me to sit there. Finally, I said, "I don't know where to start." The counselor asked a few questions and I was off and running. I was angry with my parents for not fixing this thing with school. They fixed everything else—why couldn't they fix this? When I talked to the counselor, I told him I felt I had to hide the real me. I explained that I felt trapped, as if there were a "me" who people saw and a "self" that only I knew. This

32

was the hardest part for me to explain. My "self" knew everything, could figure things out with the best coping strategies I have ever seen. The problem stemmed from the "self" not being able to tell "me" things to share with the rest of the world. People dealt with "me" on a daily basis. "Me" had to be very clever at hiding and dodging situations that could be embarrassing. "Me" would say, "No, I don't want any help" when "self" was saying, "Get a little help and I can figure it out from there." I became a little schizoid. But I have always thought of this as a coping strategy that kept me out of trouble.

This is also the time I questioned just how smart I really was. I had a full battery of tests done, but I didn't believe the counselor's interpretation of the results. He told me that I was above average in intelligence and had superior performance scores. "Yeah, right," was my comment. He then got an outside evaluator to explain the test results to me and for the first time in my life I realized I was smart. I had the tests to prove to myself that I could indeed dare to dream of bigger and better things. Now there was a new pressure. If I was smart then I had better do well. There were no more excuses. Why could I not read and write like everyone else? This was the hardest concept of all to get through my mind. I learn differently, and I had learned to cope very well. Does everyone cope in the same way? No, because we don't have the same experiences, and we learn through our failures. What we fail at depends on how we learn to cope. From these experiences we build our coping strategies. These strategies are unique to each of us.

I remember learning coping strategies in my first real job in a factory making filaments for light bulbs. I went around and put the wire into the machines. When I was not attending to a machine, I would watch the men change motors, tear down a machine, recalibrate parts, and put the machine back together. One day when I went to work early, I noticed there was a new job posted on the board, five steps above the position I held. It was a job that I had watched the men do. Knowing I could perform all the duties, I put my name on the sheet. People would not talk to me, have break, or have lunch with me. I had no idea what I had done. I felt I had committed some crime and could not, for the life of me, figure out what the crime had been. In the restroom, one of my friends told me about the rules of signing up for jobs. Women could not sign up for a level above a five. When I asked her why, she stated that it was just not done. I explained to her I could do the job and it paid a lot more money. She said that it did not matter, and I would get the cold shoulder until I took my name off the list. This, of course, made me all the more determined to keep my name on the list. After a week, the personnel manager called me into his office and explained the rules to me. When I asked him the reason, he had no answer. Several days later he told me they had instituted a new policy and I (along with the others who signed up) would have to take a test. The person having the highest score and best work record would get the job. My first thought was that I would at least be able to save face. I also wondered if this test was legal, but thought I should perhaps keep this thought to myself, feeling I was in considerable trouble already.

The next day, they put us all in a little room and gave us the test. To my surprise and delight, it was like no test I had ever seen. There were questions such as, "If you are in a small plane and the plane has an engine on each wing and the left engine stops, which way does the plane turn?" All the questions were similar and I thought, because it was so easy, it was some kind of joke. The next day, the personnel manager called me in and told me this was my last chance to reconsider my decision. Having nothing to lose (or so I thought), I said my decision stands. Having gotten a 98 on the test, the highest grade, I now had a new job. I was to report to my supervisor first thing on Monday morning and my training would start. Excited, Monday morning I did as I was told and found the supervisor. He was surrounded by everyone in the department. They cast their eyes downward and became quiet as I approached. After my greetings, to which the supervisor did not respond, he walked me to a machine, told me to change the motor, and handed me a new one to install. I had one hour to do this and if the job was not accomplished, I could pick up my paycheck on the way out. He walked back to the group. I began to work. After forty minutes I had the motor changed. The new one was installed and I started the machine. Later, I learned that the "new" motor he had given me was defective. Because it didn't work, I stripped the machine, took the motor off, went to the stock cage and asked for a new motor—one that was still sealed in its box. The man behind the counter told me there were no new motors, he would have to order one. For the first time in years, my temper took over and I was over the counter in a flash. I had him by the shirt, telling him to find one within the next few seconds or else. After I let him go, he scampered down the aisle and came back with a new motor in a sealed box. Thanking him, I climbed back over the counter and returned to my machine. With two or three minutes of installation, the machine was up and running.

I had a migraine for three days afterwards but I had a job. Soon, other women began signing up for higher levels, and they all began to talk to me again. Looking back I realized that I had missed many of the social cues as well as the unwritten rules. Although the rules needed to be changed, I am not sure I would have purposely set out to change the organization.

Another situation came up while I worked for a bank. I had been there seven years and management called me into the office on a Friday afternoon, excited about offering me a promotion. On Monday, not being able to handle their praise, their confidence in me, or my doubts about having to read and write more material, I handed in my resignation. It never occurred to me to handle this situation any other way. There was only one way out. I am not sure even now if I could have had any other response to this situation. All I could manage were thoughts and feelings of self-protection and survival. While in school I had felt trapped, so I had to protect myself from the inside. The outside, the part exposed to the world, would have to take care of itself. But now that I was on my own, I could retreat to safety. I could find a job not requiring me to read or write. Without explanation, I was out of the bank in two weeks, and on my way to another new adventure.

Next, I would start my own photography business. I had all the equipment and I enjoyed all aspects of photography. Maybe this was the answer: to be my own boss. Well, working with people was wonderful; I can get along with just about anyone. Taking pictures is an art form, and I excel at it. If I had been away from taking pictures for a while it took a while to get reacquainted with the equipment, but the artistry is always there. However, the business end of this job left a lot to be desired. Collecting money was not something I was very good at, nor was I good at saying "no" to people. I still have problems in both areas. Because of this, the photography business lasted about two years before I ran out of money. During this time I had several part-time jobs in back-up computer work. After this things began to change, bringing me to a new chapter in my life and in this book.

COMMENTARY

Typical of people with learning disabilities, Dayle tried a number of jobs and, although she did well, she considered herself a failure because of her poor reading and writing skills. At that time, she had not developed—or didn't understand—that she had the strategies necessary to succeed after she was promoted at the bank. Her reaction was to quit and find another job that did not require the skills she lacked. We can sympathize with her feelings of fear and failure—she now knew that the disabilities that had hindered her in school would not disappear. These learning disabilities were very instrumental in preventing her from climbing the ladder of success.

Dayle's varied employment background and her persistence with obtaining further education are notable to her story. She is fortunate in that she is able to hold jobs successfully; she is limited only by her perception that she cannot advance in a chosen field because her employer will discover her reading and writing weaknesses. Because she has some strong nonacademic skills, Dayle has been successful as a photographer and as a carpenter. Her determination to become an academic success and her skills with young people continually brought her back to higher education so that she could become a teacher.

It is important for people with learning disabilities as well as those who share their lives to support nonacademic endeavors and accept that technology can be a help, a strategy, for overcoming spelling, grammar, and math weaknesses. Our schools and society are far too likely to validate young people's worth and potential on the basis of their reading, writing, and math skills—exclusive of what they can do with their hands and imagination. How often do we hear that a person with poor basic (academic) skills will never make it into any of the jobs of leadership in the work force!

For Dayle, and undoubtedly for other individuals with learning disabilities, professional counseling was an important strategy in coping with the problems of real or perceived failure. Her fears of revealing her learning problems on the job forced her to seek out a counselor who helped her understand her disability and provided her with very helpful problem solving skills. As is typical of the person with a learning disability, Dayle is a concrete thinker and tends to see choices she has to make as black or white. Either she can do the job or she can't. At the time, she didn't understand that she could set small goals for herself that would eventually lead to the major goal. She needed instruction in setting realistic goals and in problem solving. Since she had not obtained those skills in school, she needed to learn how to problem solve as she faced vocational decisions. Counseling from a professional who understood the effects of learning disabilities on the psyche was helpful in getting Dayle started on developing strategies for herself.

Appendix A describes strategies suggested in this section—counseling, self-advocacy (see advocating for oneself), and social/emotional.

6

The College Years
Creating File Cabinets in my Sleep

REFLECTION

Have you ever done something in your life without knowing why you wanted to do it in the first place? I always wanted to get an education, partly because I wanted everyone else to know that I was smart and could get good grades. Years later, I learned I needed the education for me, to prove to myself I was smart, and could get good grades.

I was working at a bank when a friend of mine called and told me that if I took three more classes, I could receive an associate's degree. But, you know me: I wondered what the catch was, what tests I would have to pass, and what grade point average (GPA) I would need to complete the degree. She convinced me to continue and to take the three classes necessary. I did not need to take any tests. Finally, I took enough classes and had a 2.7 GPA. I received my general associate's degree in science in the spring of 1984 at the Technical Institute in Concord, New Hampshire.

During that winter I applied to a college in southern New Hampshire. I had an appointment to talk to Dr. Trumbull, one of the faculty members in special education. She asked me to bring a writing sample with me to the interview. Dr. Trumbull greeted me at the door of her office. We had a forty-five-minute conversation. I don't have the foggiest idea what we discussed. Then she stood up and asked me to follow her. As we walked, I was thinking, "I can't believe I ever thought I could be accepted into a four-year college. Why have I put myself in this humiliating position? She's going to show me to the door and tell me to get lost. Why did I do this to myself?" We continued to walk up stairs, down corridors, and straight into the admissions office. Dr. Trumbull told a nice young man that I could be accepted on a provisional basis. I could take up to twelve credits and, if I carried a *B* average or better, I would be accepted without provision.

Off I went to college! The first year, I had to take all the required classes, which taxed my memory. All the tests were multiple choice, fill in the blanks, and/or short answer. It was a horrible experience. I remember one specific incident. I had three major exams in one day. The first test went well. I had all my files in order, in my mind. Recall that I think of my memory as a large file cabinet, with everything I learn in a specific file. During an exam I go to the file cabinet and pull out the information located in a folder and throw the folder in a pile to be put back later. So, as you can imagine, during the second test some of the information I needed was in the pile. But what's worse, I was also adding to the already large stack of unfiled folders. I just barely finished the second test on time. Off I went to the third exam. Again, information I needed was stacked unfiled in a huge pile in my mind. I could not find the information I needed to complete the test. I needed to sleep, because when I sleep, folders are organized back into the file cabinet. I don't know how this happens, but it does. Before I went home, I stopped by Dr. Trumbull's office with my books in hand. As I dumped the books into her wastebasket, I told her she could take them and do what ever she wanted with them. Then, I turned and walked away. I went home to get the much-needed sleep. When I woke, I realized it was time to go to my next class. The books I needed were in Dr. Trumbull's office. How was I going to get them back after making a fool of myself? Walking down the hall to her office, I rehearsed all sorts of things to say. My scenarios were sad excuses. I hung around her office, hoping for some inspiration. When she came to the doorway with my books in her hands, she looked at me and said, "I thought you might need these. If you would like to talk about it sometime, let me know." I grabbed the books, thanked her, and left. How was I ever going to explain the file cabinet in my mind to a professor? But eventually I did explain—and she actually understood.

Another experience I had that year was in art history class. I figured this was going to be one of those easy A classes. The class was held in a large lecture hall. There was a screen hanging front and center. The professor showed slides one after another, and provided us with details about the artist, period, and the painting itself. I always sat in the front, to the right-hand side of the screen. I never missed a class. After each class, I pretended that I was a reporter and had to summarize each picture for the public. I walked to my next class, reciting pertinent information to the public. I had made snapshots of each picture in my mind after reciting the information (if I could say the information out loud, I would remember it). Then, into a file it would go for safekeeping. The night before the final exam, I came down with a twelve-hour bug. I was up all night, sick. I woke up late the next morning, and had to hurry to make it to the exam. When I got there, my usual seat was taken. I had to sit in the back, on the left. We were going to be shown five pictures. We were to write all the pertinent information for each picture in a blue book. Each picture would be on the screen for fifteen minutes. Up went the first picture. For me, it was as though I was looking at this picture for the first time! What was I going to do? I could recall nothing and I began to panic. I decided if I was going to flunk this test, I was going to figure out what was going on in my mind. I shut my eyes. In my mind I began to look in my files to see if I could make a match with the picture on the screen. I found that if, in my mind's eye, I put myself in the seat up front on the right, I could recall the information I needed to complete the questions.

That day, I learned why I always sat in the same seat. I make pictures in my mind and I remember what the professor says. If students ask questions, I remember who asked and who answered the question. If I have two classes in the same classroom, I sit in two different locations. This way, I am able to keep the information separate.

During my practicum in special education, one of my assignments was to keep a journal. I was also responsible for producing lesson plans, writing papers, taking tests, and giving oral reports. I decided on my own to give one of these assignments up because I just could not do everything. The journal would have to go. We were to write experiences in our journal that we had during our time in school, and reflect on those experiences. Every day was just too much for me to handle. Dr. Trumbull met with each of us at the end of the semester. Finally it was my turn. I went into her office. I had received an *A* on all my assignments. The only missing piece was my journal. She wanted to see it, so I handed her my notebook. She sat back in her chair and opened the cover. I had written some smart ditty about choosing not to do this particular assignment. She flipped through the remaining blank pages. I could just imagine what was going on in her mind. I sat quietly, waiting. She closed the notebook, blinked, and stared at me. She said, "Dayle, do you know how many points this journal is worth? Why did you choose not to do this assignment?" I answered, "I just could not look at writing one more thing every single day. But if you would like to know anything about any experience I had, I would be glad to tell you about it." She replied, "You had an *A* in this class but because this counted for so much I am going to have to give you an *AB.*" I was so excited that she didn't flunk me I almost jumped up and hugged her. I would have settled for much less. To this day, Dr. Trumbull requests practicum students to bring their journals to seminars on a weekly basis. She does look to see if the pages are blank.

As an undergraduate, I had to take a class in literacy and reading. As a part of the class, I had to take a phonics test. Each student had to receive a score of 85 or better on the phonics test to pass, even with an A on all the other assignments. We could take the test as many times as we needed to. The first time I took the test, I received a 34! I had no idea what some of the questions were, never mind the answers. About three weeks later, I took the test again and received a 68. At this rate, I could flunk this class. I got a tutor and began at the beginning. This was much too slow for me, so I began to memorize the pre- and post-tests in the book. There were over one hundred questions on those tests. With two weeks left in the semester, I had an A in all my other assignments. Again, panic started to set in. I needed to pass that test! Again, I took the test. I received a 96, got an A in the class and ended up not knowing any more about phonics than when the class started. I thanked God for my great memory.

A course called Elementary Methods comes after practicum and before student teaching in the education curriculum. It's an important class because students who can't or don't want to continue are weeded out at this time. I had a good GPA and was an older student. On paper, I looked great, for the first time in my life. Ms. Methods was my instructor. She was excited to have me as a student. I was also assigned to a pre-first classroom designed for students who had completed kindergarten but were not ready for first grade. During the first part of the course, we took a reading, spelling, and math test. I passed the reading and math test. But I had the lowest grade on the spelling test. Ms. Methods was no longer enamored with me. She called me into her office to discuss my grades, and suggested that I find another profession. I jumped out of the chair and told her that I was going to teach, I was going to take methods here or somewhere else, and then I asked her who gave her the right to play God with my life. Needless to say, we had a rather rocky relationship from that time on. I felt that my performance in the classroom had to be better than great. The pressure to perform was on, and this was the first time I felt the pressure to pave the way for other student with learning disabilities. If I failed, would I close the door to those who followed me? The ramifications were too great for me to think about. I just had to be better than all the other students in the classroom, and you know what? I was! I received a score of 100 in the teaching part of the assessment. My final grade was AB; not bad for someone who can't spell.

This was also the class in which I had a significant experience with a research paper. I wrote the paper and passed it in on time. That night, one of the school athletes came to my apartment and asked if I could help her with her paper for the same class. Her schedule was tight, and she was so tired that she fell asleep on the couch. So, I wrote the paper and she handed it in the next day. I received a C on mine and she received an A. Interesting, don't you think? I felt my paper got a lower grade because the teacher expected less of me. I have not gotten over this yet. When I read papers today I never look at who has written it until after I have commented and graded the paper. I learned a lot of lessons in that class, some positive and others that raised major questions about the way students with disabilities are treated in class.

In the spring of 1986, I applied to both the University of Virginia and Keene State College to work on a master's degree. I was accepted at both institutions. I chose Keene State because the school offered me a teaching assistantship. Of all the schooling I've had, this was the most fun. There were many reasons for this, the most important of which was that I got to take all the classes I truly enjoyed. I also worked with college students who had learning disabilities. I did presentations in classes, workshops, conferences, and schools around the state on what it's like to be a student with a learning disability. There were no exams in my courses, only presentations and papers. I visited the schools to observe and learn different teaching techniques. I had fun both as a student and as a teacher. My GPA for graduation was 3.73—not bad for anyone, let alone a student with reading and writing problems. Without the coping strategies I developed along the way, the story would have been quite different. For instance, in exchange for dinners, I asked a friend to type the final drafts of my papers and correct the punctuation and spelling. When I had a research paper to write, I engaged each of my professors in conversations about the topic I had chosen. These people love to talk about what they know! I got all sorts of good information, along with the names of the references they thought were the best. I was saved having to read all the references in the library on the topic and gathered much information from my chats with each teacher! As a graduate assistant, I could determine each professor's biases, and could focus the content of each paper toward a particular belief system.

COMMENTARY

For Dayle, these years were indeed fun. Through the years, she had developed academic strategies that worked well for her. Many of the strategies she described in the Reflection above as being necessary to complete her college assignments. As a greater number of students with learning disabilities are accepted to college, the need for strategies is receiving greater recognition from both students and faculty.

At this educational stage, learned helplessness becomes an almost insurmountable impediment to academic success. This term has come to mean the inability of the individual with the disability to develop strategies for success. It can be traced back to well-meaning special education teachers or parents who, by their own actions, have taught students to rely on others to do the work for them. It happens because a teacher or parent does not want a student to fail. However, the outcome is that individuals with learning problems become helpless and unable to develop strategies for themselves. We need to recognize that there is more than one way to succeed in academic subjects, and that the individual should be taught to use any strengths to succeed. The idea, long favored in special education, that academic weaknesses must be strengthened in order for a student to be successful, is no longer considered to be the only way he or she can be taught. That approach arose from the medical model, which focuses on diagnosis and curing the illness. In learning disabilities, the weakness, though it may be strengthened, is still a detriment to efficient learning (Ariel, 1992). An individual's strengths need to be identified and then used as an aid to overcoming the problem. Dayle has become extremely adept at using her own strengths. She used her powerful visual memory as an aid to learning in the art history class, and her ability to converse with her professors to narrow the research topics and do the library research necessary to complete a topic. Her strengths with the computer, spelling and grammar checks, and eventually a friend who could read her document and point out any problems in her writing (so *she* could correct them), made it possible for Dayle to succeed far beyond academic expectations.

Instead of doing the work for a person with a learning disability, it is important to help him or her find ways to use strengths as a way to overcome problems and thus complete the work alone. Recognize that there is more than one way to teach any subject. Let a student with a writing problem use art or strong verbal skills to demonstrate what he or she knows about a subject. This book has mentioned many strategies that Dayle developed. Each student, however, will need to be taught strategies that work for him or her; thus, the teacher and student must work together to develop strategies.

In this Reflection, Dayle mentions how tired she became when the academic demands become too much for her to manage. This fatigue is not an indication of laziness; it is true exhaustion. Students with learning disabilities often need more rest than other students. What seems to many of us like a simple academic task may require tremendous effort on the part of a person like Dayle.

Obviously, Dayle can accomplish what other people with her level of education can. The expectations of her should not have differed from those of other college students. Lowering expectations is another mistake teachers and parents often make with children with learning disabilities. Different ways of teaching, and academic assignments that require the same outcomes for everyone are necessary; but lowering standards *is not*. Instead, the teacher must be flexible enough to understand that there are many ways to meet the desired standard. No one has to complete a fifty-page paper to prove that he or she can write correctly. If the topic chosen requires a fifty-page paper to do it justice, then help the student find strategies to complete the assignment and/or understand that he or she may need extra time to complete the written assignment. If the purpose of the assignment is to prove that a student understands the topic, allow him or her to present the information in a nonwritten format.

7

Letter to Self
The Road to the Dream

REFLECTION

Dear Self,

This has been one of the worst and best years of my life. I was accepted by the University of Connecticut and there was a good chance I would be able to attend in the fall. I worked out all the logistics, saved money, handed in my resignation and said good-bye to my family and friends. I intended to reach for the stars. This chance to work for my doctorate was my unattainable dream. I should not have been accepted in the first place. No, that's not right. I should not have gotten my master's, my bachelor's, or even my associate's degrees. That's what I was told all those years ago. It amazes me that of all the things to remember, I should remember the negative things such as, "You will never," "You can not," "You're not able to." Do I remember only the negative? Maybe I just never heard the positive because people didn't want me to get my hopes up just to fail again. Well here I am, years later, and I have just successfully completed the first semester of my doctoral program. Now, just what am I supposed to do with all this information I have gained? It does not register right in my heart or mind. It should make me feel great and wonderful. But no one prepared me for success and I am not sure how to handle it. It feels good, yet I am so afraid! Of what, I am not sure. I was all set to fail because that's what I always do in an academic situation. I even tried not to study so that I would know what to do. I did not fail, so now what do I do? I can't possibly start a second semester of a doctoral program. This is my dream and I am in it. I don't think I should be here. I don't have a new dream, for this has always been my dream. I can't be or do better than this. Have I gone so far beyond my potential that I am lost? Is there no way back to the safety of failure? No one has ever prepared me for this kind of success. I always heard

44

the words, "You can do or be anything you want to be," but in my heart and mind the words were always translated into, "You can do or be anything you want to be but there are a lot of things you can't do, so make sure your goals are not set too high." So, I would say one thing out loud, but in my mind, getting my doctorate was always my secret goal. The secret is out and I am lost in a world of dark wonder with no direction, no light, no boundaries! The feeling is worse now because, since I've made it this far, how bad can this learning disability be? Certainly not too bad. Since I've been at U. Conn., I have been in a state of heightened awareness, ready for anything from any direction to attack and annihilate me into oblivion. I can't talk to my professors because they see my bewilderment as a weakness and my sense of failure as an old coping skill. What they don't understand is this new absolutely wonderful feeling I have, but don't know what it is or how to explain it. Why do I put myself into this mess? How can I stand to feel so bad and so good at the same time? Why does it not kill me? The good is the best and the bad is the worst I have ever experienced, and they live inside me at the same time. I can't go on like this, with no harmony and no goals. I can't form a goal because now there seems to be no ceiling and the success is somehow connected with the bad feelings. I don't understand why. I wish there was a way to explain how I sometimes feel. It's like I felt when I was a child, yet with so much more intensity than in those early years. Could it be that the potential success is so great that it makes the failure that much more devastating? I wonder. I want so much to have the power to alleviate this inner suffering in children. No one should have to go through this lonely kind of hell. Thank you, Self, for letting this out. Maybe now I can deal with whatever this feeling is.

COMMENTARY

The psychological turmoil that individuals with learning disabilities experience is one of the most poorly understood aspects of the disability. In all the definitions, the disability is said to be due to psychological processing or central nervous system dysfunctions. It is manifested by significant difficulties in acquisition or use of oral language, reading, writing, reasoning, or mathematical abilities. The disability may occur concomitantly with other handicapping conditions—including emotional disturbance—but these conditions are not *basic* to the learning disability.

Professionals in the field of learning disabilities generally recognize the concomitant nature of emotional problems. However, remediation techniques generally focus on the academic weaknesses. The belief is that the student who learns how to cope with the learning disability will, in that process, overcome the emotional problems that occur because of it. This practice does not consider the possibility that emotional and other psychological problems may, in and of themselves, be a part of the learning disability. Several researchers today suggest that the psychosocial problems of the learning-disabled individual must be approached directly, as are the academic problems of the individual with a learning disability (Gerber, Ness, and Price, 1990; Ryan and Price, 1992).

In this Reflection, Dayle's emotional reactions appear to be a result of her battle with learning disabilities throughout her school and work years. As an adult, however, they are an integral part of who she is, and her fears of success and of failure are certainly concomitants to the learning problems. Academically, she has gone further than anyone, including herself, ever thought possible. What if she actually succeeds in the doctoral program? The reading and writing problems will still be there! What if she obtains the job she wants, helping children "alleviate this inner suffering," and is discovered to have a learning disability? She has reached the pinnacle, only to be rudely knocked off because the academic problems are still there.

It is no wonder that Dayle is frightened by her success, and questions whether she should try harder to do what is most comfortable to her—fail. The coping strategy demonstrated in this Reflection is the writing of the Reflection itself. Dayle does a good job of pinpointing her feelings by writing about them. Verbalizing how she feels seems to help her understand what she is going through. The written-language problems do not interfere because she is talking to herself. She is, in a sense, keeping a diary.

Appendix A describes counseling as a strategy as suggested in this Reflection (see also reflection on counseling).

8

Letter to Self
Tired of the Fight

REFLECTION

Dear Self,

Well self here I am again! Your probably wondering what it is this time, right? Here goes. You remember last spring when I drove myself to UCONN all by myself and for the first time on a day when I had an appointment. Well this Wed. I have to do a workshop in Cranston RI and I've never been there. I'am not worried about the workshop but getting there is a real threat. No one in the world would understand this but you because I'am too busy worring about the road signs. But it dosen't worrie me to talk for $2\frac{1}{2}$ hours.

    This thing I have that they call a learning disability I never asked for and I don't want. I thought it had gone away because I diden't have to deel with it for such a long time . Here it is again its like having a full blown case of the measles. You can't get away from it. Like the tar baby! Like a canser. Its so hard to deal with because I am the only one that knows I have to deal with it. Its inside and I cant quiet the pain. I have it and I don't want it and its too dam bad, its there to stay, deal with it, face it, let it go. I dont want to deal with it any more I'am tired, of the fight. Every thing is so much work. Every day all day all there is work, just to stay alive. Self do you have any idea what kind of concintration it takes to live a day in my life? Do you? Your so stuped some times your out there smiling at every one talking like you know what your doing and here I am working my brains out trying to make you look good. Well Iam tired. The worst part is that I like you and I do give a dam if you look good. Yet you always hide me. Know one knows I exist and lately the pain is so powerful that it hurts almost all the time now.

47

Well self your such an ass hole no one knows that I dont know how to get to Cranston and you just go about looking good while I have to do all the work once again. I do have to admit that you do make it funny some times and I do have to lauff (l-a-f) laugh so there see your not so smart. My Franklin speller helps once in a while. It didn't know what lauff was so I put in lauph and it found laugh. You see what I have to go through you meat head. I know you had to get up and get the speller but Iam the one that has to figure everything out. Well thanks for listening by the way you need to lose some weight your not so young any more ya know. Your slow but I still like you, and you are a good listener.

COMMENTARY

The obvious signs of learning disabilities seen in this reflection are the spelling, grammar, and punctuation errors. The learning-disabled individual with a severe spelling and reading problem (in medical terms, the dyslexic) often demonstrates spelling errors that follow no pattern. The same word— or sound within a word—is not consistently misspelled the same way. More than likely, this occurs when a person does not have a visual memory for the phonemes (sounds) designated by graphemes (letters) because the sound–symbol relationship is not consistent in the spelling of English words. There are many possibilities for the spelling of the word *laugh*; "laff" is what the word sounds like, but the spelling could be "laf" or "lauff," or even "laph," since *ph* sounds like *f*.

Although the person with a learning disability may use correct grammar in speaking, this skill may not carry over into written language. Researchers believe that correct grammar develops in children as they use and listen to language during the preschool years (Chomsky, 1957; Bloom and Lahey, 1978; Bernstein and Tiegerman, 1993). However, this development does not seem to happen as smoothly in many children with learning disabilities (Wiig and Semel, 1984). The translation from spoken to written language presents special problems for the learning disabled since it is based on listening, talking, handwriting, reading, and spelling skills. Dayle demonstrates problems in several of those basic skills, so it is no wonder that her disability is exhibited in written composition.

Punctuation often seems to make no sense to the writer with learning disabilities. As Dayle reports, she pauses appropriately when she reads her own writing, so why can't others do the same when they read her work? Punctuation, capitalization, and the formation of paragraphs are based on a firm understanding of word groups as sentences with beginnings and endings, of proper nouns that require capitalization, and of groups of sentences that go together. For Dayle, the entire written piece is connected. How can she then decide where paragraphs should begin and end?

In this Reflection, Dayle is thrown into a quandary because she has to take a trip to a place she has never been. She is not concerned about being able to deliver her lecture, but she is very much afraid of finding her way to the correct location. Imagine how difficult this might be for you if you needed to concentrate not only on driving over new roads but also on reading all the direction signs and route numbers. Finding your way in a car to a new location requires expertise in the techniques of driving as well as the ability to read directions quickly before they are out of sight. Dayle could not read the signs. Often, there is little time to make a decision as to which way to go. Problems with any of the prerequisite skills may result in getting hopelessly lost. Dayle's inability to read quickly and her tendency to read numbers in the wrong order would indeed result in fear as she attempted to find a new place on her own.

Combined with this fear of not being able to read the road signs is the fear of the unknown, a common problem for many people with learning disabilities. Individuals with learning disabilities need to be able to predict what is going to happen next, and often become upset if they cannot do that. Not only did Dayle consider the real possibility of never locating the school in Cranston, but she also didn't have any idea of what to expect when she got there. As we will continue to see in many of her Reflections, Dayle's anxiety about not knowing what to expect is a theme that runs through many of her experiences.

In this Reflection, Dayle speaks of the hidden quality of her disability. This characteristic, although it seems to be a benefit to the uninitiated, is often devastating because it leads others to the mistaken conclusion that there is nothing "wrong" with the individual with a learning disability. When the perfectly normal looking person cannot read or write or speak clearly, it must be because that person is not very intelligent or is not trying. But the individual with a learning disability may be very intelligent, and as Dayle states clearly, tries much harder than others to accomplish the same work. According to Mercer (1991), the discrepancy factor is considered by most authorities to be the common denominator of learning disabilities. This occurs when the achievement level of a student differs greatly from his or her academic potential. Self-esteem also suffers greatly, as is clear in Dayle's concerns about whether or not she can fool people into thinking that she is not stupid.

As is typical of individuals with learning disabilities, Dayle's disability does not affect everything she does. She is quite able to deliver a two-and-a-half-hour workshop, yet reading road signs is extremely difficult. There was a period of time when she was less affected by her disability because of the type of activities she was engaged in, but as she meets the rigors of a doctoral program, she worries about the reappearance of her learning disability. It is also clear that the underlying learning disability does not go away. The individual may develop coping strategies, but he or she continues to have unique needs at each stage of life. New strategies for compensating with the effects of the disability must be created constantly.

Appendix A describes strategies suggested in this Reflection—traveling, spelling, grammar, punctuation, and reading.

9

Letter to Self
I Am not Sure I Like Myself or You

REFLECTION

Dear Self,

Well Self, you listened last time so I thought I would give you another chance so hear goes.

Reality:
I seem to be of two minds, the one that understands what's happening to me in the educational process. How well I am doing . The logical self that has a plan, a goal. The self that thinks in terms of one day at a time yet, understands that only after the 60 weeks will the goal end. This self understands the reality of it all. Understands no matter what I can't do, that I had better figure it all out because if I don't, I will fail and self doesn't care what it takes or how long, just get it done and go on.

Intuition:
The other self is more reflective consistently questions what is going on, is constantly aware of all others around me. Knows what temperature it is if someones mood changes. Intuitively knows what is about to happen. This self is the best anticipator I've ever known and is almost always tired.

I'am not sure I like either self in and of its self. Why do they have to be so separate? are they stronger separate? Why are they in such conflict all the time? Why can't I let go of them or just relax around them. Why do I have to be so rigid it interferes with so much of my life. Why do I even think about all this? Is it because myselves are so separate? Yet, could this be why I also succeed in an academic world which is so foreign to me.

51

The reason I am writing this is because its almost time for me to go back to school and my chest hurts again. Why? I fluctuate from feeling so strong to a fattial insecurity, its the extremes that hurt.

I met with a young man ,12, I believe, and so much pain came back. He can't read it's not that he can read a little he can't read at all. Which brought up all the things we do to kids like why are we continuing to stuff reading down his throat. Why aren't we teaching him how to cope (too) I am not saying stop the reading I say stop the cramming and teach other things like using his memory, make him aware of all the other skills he needs to develop because if we don't do this he will not be able to function. I don't know when I became aware of the things I do but there are a lot of them like memorizing places I need to know or go. Making maps in my head making attachments to experiences I've had so that I can remember what the class is about. Making games and stories out of situations. They (the system) seem to think that mainstreaming is the answer to all things, well if your different your different and main streaming isn't going to change that so why not be different with those that are different. We send kids away to schools that cost tons of money when all we need to do is teach them differently and teach them things they need to know to cope in this world of words. Mainstreaming these students puts them in a position where they have to compete with kids that can do all the things that LD students can't do and that's supposed to be fun and a learning experience well its not. Lo kids need to be exposed to the same kinds of things but in a different way.

10

Letter to Self

I Am Always the One Who Has To Change

REFLECTION

Well, Self, here I am again,

I just got out of a doctoral seminar and I am feeling like a "nothing." I need time to think about what others in the class are saying and then try to fit it into my schema, but by the time I have formulated my thoughts, the class is on to another subject. So rather than trying to be a contributor I become a listener. At one point, after being asked what it was like to be learning disabled, I told the professor some of my frustrations in class (which I know now was a big mistake), and he said that I could do something else other than write papers.

I look at it this way. I am the one who is different, I am the one who has to do something different, and I am the one who has to come up with the way to do it. Now, Self, don't you find that interesting? The one with the fewest compensatory skills has to do something above and beyond. The professors are doing to me (again) what they do to kids every day. They are making me more different. They want me to change instead of changing their own attitudes and beliefs. If they were more open-minded, we could all experience change. So the isolation I have always felt from the rest of the group because of my disability becomes greater, and I feel even more isolated. These people are so-called experts in the field of learning disabilities, and yet they seem to know very little about what it's really like to have a learning disability. I have to struggle through reading the articles. Then I have to try to find the common theme. Then I have to sit down and write the paper. Someone has to correct my spelling, punctuation, and grammar. The reading and writing are agonizing for me. Does this mean that I should not be here? I am, I feel, being punished for not being able to complete these requirements easily. This is my disability. I would be better off if I were blind. Then people would understand and not make me do the things I can't do without a tremendous amount of effort. I don't look "disabled," and I am trying hard to hide it, but I just can't.

Look at what I've written and tell me what's not right. Is it the thought process or is it the written word? The reality is that I am the one who always has to change, and I am the one with the least amount of ability to do so. And I am the one who is different and now I am the one who has to be more so. Well, Self, I am sorry but this time I can't get the hurt out very well. These "supreme beings" still don't understand that they want me to be (as they always do) just like everyone else. They don't want me to be different because it confuses them and they can't fix me. I am an enigma to them and as much as they try to understand, they can't.

COMMENTARY

The seminar discussions are fast and confusing for Dayle. She doesn't have time to take in all the information she hears, match it to what she already thinks about the topic, and organize it all into a new schema. She tries to cope with the situation by putting all her efforts into listening and organizing rather than listening, talking, and organizing all the data. After struggling with the seminar discussion, she must write a paper about some aspect of the topic for the day. Organizing abstract thoughts presented quickly is hard enough, but to add to that the requirement of a written paper in which she must not only organize her thoughts but also spell words correctly and be grammatically correct is so much of a focus on weaknesses that Dayle panics at the mere thought of it. The entire activity seems impossible, and the feeling of failure looms. Dayle dares to approach the professor about the monumental effort of the task and is told that she can accomplish the task in some other manner.

As she says clearly, once again she feels different for she is the one who must change. For the professor and students for whom the task is challenging but possible, nothing must change—but for Dayle, as she struggles over the initial task, she must find a way to prove to everyone else that she has the information and is able to use it. This is a familiar bind for anyone with disabilities: "We're willing to let you do it in any way you can, but we are going to continue to value most the way we teach and the traditional way students show us what they learn." Dayle advocates flexibility for all the students in the classroom. Not only could she do a better job if she approaches the task differently, but other, "normal" students may also accomplish more with an alternative approach. Demonstrating that one understands a new concept is difficult enough without adding to it the requirement that there is only one acceptable way to demonstrate that knowledge.

When the disability is physical, such as blindness, teachers tend to be more understanding and teach with an eye toward making use of the student's strengths—perhaps with auditory and kinesthetic strategies. However, if a student is learning disabled, he or she must find a way to overcome her disabilities or be asked to choose a different way to prove she is obtaining the information. It is not surprising that such "understanding" on the part of a well-intentioned teacher leads to even more emotional strife.

Research may lead to a better understanding of learning disabilities, and to a variety of strategies for overcoming the problem. However, it seldom leads to an understanding of the social–emotional effects on the individual. It also does little to help an individual with learning disabilities identify strengths and learn how to capitalize on them. Dayle clearly demonstrates problems in psychosocial issues and the identification of strengths, and has found that many of her professors, who are well versed in the research, are not able to offer any real support or assistance. She alone is most aware of her weaknesses and, having learned again and again that these weaknesses are indicative of failure in our society, has developed emotional doubts about herself.

Appendix A describes strategies suggested in this reflection—inclusion, social cues (social/emotional problems), and self-advocacy (talking with the teacher).

11

The Intervening Years
Awarded a Ph. D., Now What?

REFLECTION

What happened during the years between finishing the dissertation and now? While I was still writing my heart out, I worked as the lead teacher in a school for adjudicated boys with emotional problems and/or learning disabilities. The school was a residential placement as well. The next step for these boys (eight to eighteen years of age) was either back to their home school or to the Youth Detention Center. This was a wonderful experience, and a great learning experience for me. However, I found myself in the same situation as I was in the public school system. I could not make curricular changes or institute new policies without interference from administrators. Again, the people making the decisions for students were not the ones working with them on a daily basis. Had I gone through all this, never to make a difference? Frustrated, I changed jobs and obtained a position at Keene State College as the educational coordinator for a federal grant. We were to train middle-school teachers to work with emotionally disabled students. Most of the teachers were told a week before school started that they were:

1. Now working in a fully inclusive school (no more continuum of services for special needs students)
2. Now part of a team (they had no idea what this meant)
3. In a research study with Keene State College.

In their position, I could understand why these teachers were not pleased to see us! So I struggled through another three years. However, the one bright spot was working with the family coordinator, Barbara Manning. She kept me sane and taught me a lot about the importance of family involvement in a child's schooling. We also taught a college class together at Keene State

College. Barb was wonderful to work with, and between the two of us, the students were inundated with so much information they were a little over-whelmed. They also produced outstanding projects.

Because we knew this was only a three-year project, we all started looking for new employment at about the two-and-a-half-year mark. I was lucky; I found the job of my dreams, working with wonderful, dedicated, happy people who appreciate me for who I am.

12

A University Professor

Setting New Goals

REFLECTION

Today, I am sitting in my office at the University of Wisconsin at Stevens Point. I am an assistant professor of education, and it is the most wonderful experience of my life! I teach students who are bright, enthusiastic, and willing to take chances. In the classes I teach, I have the opportunity to share my life experiences and assure them that hard work will pay off.

I have learned much about teaching from my experiences this first semester in Wisconsin. I need to be more structured than I have been in the past, and I must learn how to build more bridges from one topic to another, making transitions easier for students. I also need to hone my time-management skills since I either prepare for six hours to teach a one-hour class, or spend one hour working on a series of classes that last for six hours. I must say that as the semester has progressed, my management of time has improved. As a matter of fact, I'm finding that I have a much easier time becoming better at things than I once thought I could. Perhaps it is because I finally believe that I *can* do it!

I see my greatest strength as working with and getting along with my peers. I can honestly say this is the best job I have ever had. My colleagues are hard working, enthusiastic, and understanding professionals. They have made my transition from the East to the Midwest very comfortable. I look forward to each new day with excitement and wonder. I know that my disability is not going to disappear. There will be times when it still jumps up and grabs me by surprise. There will be people who believe I am incapable of performing at this level. As for me, I now believe the problem is theirs, not mine. I have received the gold medal of education and I now believe that I am okay. If there are people who don't understand how I made it through this educational maze, they now need to seek me out. I am free at last, and it feels great! I don't know what the future holds for me but whatever it is, I think it will be exciting. My old dream of being a student and getting an education has gone far beyond what anyone, including me, ever thought was possible. Now that I have obtained the education I so longed for, it is still difficult for me to accept it as reality and continue on to a new goal.

Accept it, I will—and begin again—but I don't think any goal will be as difficult to reach as the first one. Part of my new goal is to become the best teacher I am able to be. I envision this as a continuing goal. I would also like to touch the lives of the students who are in my classes. These students, the ones who will carry the torch and make the future decisions, are the future of our profession. By inviting my students to explore diversity of all kinds, I feel my dreams will be fulfilled. The following anonymous verse means a great deal to me as a teacher. I have changed the last word from *child* to *student*.

> One hundred years from now. . . .
> It will not matter what kind of house I lived in,
> how much I had in my bank account,
> nor what my clothes looked like.
> But the world may be a little better because I was
> important in the life of a student.

Appendix A

STRATEGIES

This appendix contains suggestions for strategies that Dayle has found valuable. We believe that many of them would be helpful for another individual with similar problems. They may also provide ideas for other strategies. From our experiences and those of many other teachers of students with learning disabilities, we have learned that there are no certainties in the education of these individuals. What works well with one student may or may not work with another, seemingly identical, student. Further, teaching techniques that work well one day may not work at all the next day with the same individual. This is due not only to the heterogeneity of the disability, but also to the differences in learning and emotional styles of the individuals themselves. Certainly, the strategies that follow are worth trying. The ideas presented may well lead to adaptations that are suitable for other children or adults with learning disabilities.

We believe that the student with learning disabilities must be a part of his or her own education if he or she is to be successful. The teacher, parent, friend, sibling, or spouse can support and provide help where necessary, but the individual with the disability must be a full-fledged partner. With support and understanding, the individual can help analyze his or her own strengths and weaknesses, and learn how to develop strategies that work. To begin, a thorough evaluation of the individual should be made, including observations in and out of the educational environment as well as the insights of a competent educational and psychological tester.

ACADEMIC EXPECTATION—See Chapter 6, Commentary

ADVOCACY (SELF)—The Ability to Tell a Teacher, an
Employer, or a Friend What It Means to You to Have a
Learning Disability

The importance of this strategy cannot be overemphasized. Many individuals with learning disabilities are unable to describe their problems to another person because they simply don't know which words to use. Saying, "I have a learning disability," or "I am dyslexic," does not help the listener. This problem originates with the medical model of disabilities, which implies that there is a meaningful name for the problem and the name will lead to a cure, much as the diagnosis of the flu leads to a prescription of medication and/or a recovery plan. The term *learning disabilities* includes many academically and socially based differences from the norm. An individual with one of these problems must be able to describe how he or she learns, or the exact nature of the problems he or she has with learning. Rather than, "I have a problem with reading," a person such as Dayle must say, "I cannot remember the phonics rules most of the time, and when I do, I become confused because of all the exceptions to the rules."

Suggestions: As a teacher or a parent, be certain that the child or adolescent you are concerned about can describe his or her learning problem to others. Have her practice by telling you and then explaining to others she doesn't know as well.

A teacher or employer may not understand the technological terms used to describe a disability. They will, however, understand an explanation of what the individual can and cannot do as a result of the disability. As a teacher, Dayle must be able to tell her students and her boss that she must use a computer with a program for spelling and grammar check, that she may make spelling mistakes when writing on the blackboard but, as long as she has an overhead projector, she can prepare the key points of her lesson on film ahead of time. Dayle has the presence and flexibility that make her an excellent teacher. She has the skills to involve her class members in constructive ways. They often become a part of the strategy she needs. For instance, students become note takers and board writers, they learn how to use a thesaurus to find synonyms if word recall becomes a problem, and they become adept at reading challenging material and, in small groups, summarizing it for the rest of the class.

Help the student with a learning disability understand his or her strengths and use them as strategies for getting through difficult times. A highly developed sense of humor is a wonderful strategy!

ANTICIPATION—Learning How to Anticipate

Anticipation is using observation skills and memory of similar situations to determine ahead of time what is likely to happen in a new situation. Anticipation is useful because Dayle cannot prepare herself for a new situation by reading about it or listening to someone tell her about it. She needs to engage in experience in order to learn well, and she needs time to compare what she thinks might happen with past experiences. Through observing people carefully, she has learned how they react in certain types of situations. She has learned how to read body language and other nonverbal means of communication. By remembering and visualizing the actual past experience, she can relate it to the new experience and avoid having to quickly rely on a book or other written account of the demands of the activity.

Suggestions: Provide time for the person to talk about the activity he or she will be involved in and to relate the new experience to past, similar ones. Simulate the new experience (moving into or out of a special class or individual tutoring, a job interview, the first day on a job, interacting with others at a party, and so forth) ahead of time. Encourage the individual (or accompany him or her) to visit a new class, a new dorm, an interview or appointment site, ahead of the time she is scheduled to be there. Draw a map and talk through the directions for traveling to a new place.

CATEGORIZATION—The Ability to Put Objects and Ideas into Groups with Similar Attributes

Categorization is determining the similarities between individual things and placing them together because of these similarities. For instance, knowing that a cow, a lion, a mouse, and a snake all have similarities and thus placing them all in the category called animals. Categorization is used for organizing information so that it can be retrieved easily during the thinking process. The learner needs to be able to categorize and then generalize it to specific situations. In many of her reflections, Dayle speaks of the great difficulty she has in remembering everything. She keeps "files" in her mind that she uses to store each item, skill, or idea. For instance, reading has many files; one for reading in reading class, one for social studies reading, and one for science. It took Dayle far longer than the normal learner to grasp the fact that reading is reading, wherever it occurs.

Suggestions: See the strategy on generalization for a clearer view of how categorization and generalization work together.

Give students objects that they can categorize; for instance, blocks of different colors and shapes. Then have them identify one attribute that is similar about the objects. Some will categorize by color, others by shape. Still another category could be the material of which the blocks are composed (wood, plastic). This activity will provide practice in categorizing and in recognizing that there can be more than one category for the same items.

Have the students organize objects or ideas according to a category, then give them another categorical group and ask them to name the similar characteristic of each group. Another category may arise from this generalization. For instance, the students organize toy animals into pets and farm animals; the teacher provides a set of wild animals. As they discuss the similarities between the groups, the students will begin to gain an appreciation of the general category of animal kingdom.

Demonstrate how biologists have organized all living things into plant and animal kingdoms, which are then broken into genus, species, and so forth. This can lead to a discussion of the helpfulness of categories and to student participation in organizing concrete categories that can, in turn, be generalized to far more abstract categories.

COUNSELING—Finding a Trained Person to Talk with About the Psychosocial and Emotional Problems Associated with the Learning Disability

Counseling is useful because the basic skill deficiencies that accompany a learning disability make the problem seem to hinder almost every activity in which the individual becomes involved. These basic skills are the background of much that is academic, and school failure results in the person feeling that he or she is a failure in all aspects of life. Dayle equates this failure with being a bad person. Failure and being bad, then, becomes the pervasive mood of each day. A good counselor, who is knowledgeable about the effects of a disability, can help the person sort out strengths from weaknesses, bad from good, and provide suggestions for coping with the disability.

Suggestions: Advocate for the availability of counseling as a part of the Individual Education Plan (IEP) for every child with a disability in the schools. Merely knowing that such a person is available to talk with is often enough support for some individuals with learning disabilities.

Choose a counselor with a track record that includes working with people with learning disabilities, or who is known to have the skills to do so.

Discuss with the individual reasons for talking with a counselor, and together devise a plan for meeting and talking with the counselor. If the student does not want to see a counselor, make sure he or she understands that the option is available at any time and doesn't have to be used immediately. For some interesting ideas and strategies integral to her reflections, see Dayle's "Reflection on Employment."

DIARY (KEEPING ONE)—See Chapter 7, Commentary

GENERALIZATION—Learning How to Generalize Information

Generalization is understanding how the specific facts one has learned about an event or place may be related to other events or places. Gaining the ability to build categories of related information is useful because most people with learning disabilities have trouble generalizing information they have learned to other similar situations. Dayle recites her problems with generalizing information about Exeter, New Hampshire. Since a major component of learning disabilities is the characteristic of thinking in concrete terms rather than abstract terms, this cognitive skill must be developed. When asked how she thinks about a category filled with many items, such as birds, Dayle responds that she visualizes all the different species of bird she knows; then, when asked how all birds are alike, she visualizes such characteristics as color, nesting habits, food, and migration habits of each of the birds in her mind. She does not think of the category of birds in the abstract—warm-blooded animals with wings and feathers, the characteristic most people attribute to all creatures in this class. When asked the question, "How are an apple and an orange alike?" Dayle responds, "You can eat them both, they both have peels, and they are round." Only later does she speak of the major characteristic that defines the class: "They are both fruits."

Suggestions: When he or she is facing a new task, remind the individual that not everything about the task is new. For instance, the multiplication tables learned for multiplication are used also in division. The reading that one does for science or social studies involves the same reading skills that one uses in reading class. (A whole new set of skills is not required for reading in each subject.) People with learning disabilities in this area do not automatically think in abstract terms or generalize information. However, they can be taught to do so.

Have students and adults place concrete items in categories. Then talk about the characteristic of each item and how it compares to the characteristics of other items in the category.

Play similarities games with visual objects and words. For instance, use pictures of common objects and ask the individual how they are alike. Discuss characteristics of the objects, but also discuss the class or category that similar objects belong to. Play the same game with words.

Play thinking games. For instance, ask the individual to describe the similarities between one-fourth of a cup, one-fourth of a room, one-fourth of an inch, and one-fourth of a pie. Are they all the same size? Why or why not?

Do not expect all individuals with learning disabilities to be able to memorize abstract material, even if they have good memories. They remember well because they can relate the abstract to very concrete images. Make sure abstract ideas on tests relate to something in the individual's own experience.

GOAL SETTING—Deciding upon at Least One Specific Accomplishment for the Future

Goal setting must be something the individual really wants to do (obtaining a Ph.D. in Dayle's case) and may not seem realistic to anyone else. It is useful because it provides a direction for effort.

Suggestions: Talk to the individual about what he or she really wants to do in the future. Ask how he or she might reach that goal. Together, plan steps toward reaching the goal. These steps may be very small and it should be clear exactly how the steps will be approached. Provide on-going support and encouragement. If need be, work together to break a step down even further. Above all, do *not* accomplish the step for the individual or insinuate in any way that the disability is too great a detriment toward reaching the goal.

GRAMMAR—See Punctuation

INCLUSION—When Students with Special Needs are Totally Assimilated into the Regular Education Classes

Inclusion is useful because students with special needs are treated as equals and the other students experience the exceptional needs of disabled individuals. In short, inclusion represents society.

Suggestions: We believe that there should be a continuum of services, with the final goal being that students with special needs will be totally assimilated in the regular classroom. Each student should be treated on an individual basis and moved along the continuum as fast as possible for that individual.

LEARNED HELPLESSNESS—See Chapter 6, Commentary

MEMORY—Using Memory Strengths

Memory problems are common among individuals with learning disabilities. The student may have difficulty remembering symbols such as letters, numbers, or even words. He or she may remember something one day and not the next. Using memory strengths is useful because an individual's memory for abstractions (matching a sound with symbol as in learning to read by phonics or remembering what symbols go together in order to spell correctly) may not be good. This is the case with Dayle. However, she has an excellent memory for remembering things that have innate meaning, whether she receives them visually or auditorily. When asked to spell the word *elephant*, Dayle sees the animal in her mind, not the letters that together spell the word correctly. For an individual like Dayle, this ability to visualize objects and events is a strength, and he or she should be taught how to use it.

Suggestions: Use visual images as a regular part of teaching. For instance, when teaching the Civil War, use drawings and films of major events. Describe what is happening, using the pictures. Leave the pictures or films available so that the individual can view them at his or her leisure. It is important to keep these visual images in sequence (number them) since organization can be such a problem for the person with a learning disability.

In a classroom setting, be certain that the student with a learning disability sits in the same location every day. Observing what is being seen and heard from the same perspective day by day is a necessary strategy for Dayle and many individuals with similar problems.

ORGANIZATION—See Categorization

PROBLEM-SOLVING SKILLS—The Possession of Skills That Allow a Person to Analyze a Problem, Devise Possible Solutions, and Make a Choice About Which Solution to Try

Problem-solving skills have only recently become a focus in school because of the recognition that too much reliance on rote memorization does not facilitate effective problem solving. Many students, particularly those with learning disabilities, must be taught how to solve problems. They do not simply absorb the skill when faced with day by day problems.

Suggestions: Observe a problem the individual is having that is effecting success in completing something important. It could be a social problem, an academic problem, and so forth. Ask, "What is the problem you are having?" Help the individual state the problem concretely. Ask, "What are some of the possible solutions?" Ask, "What are the consequences of each of your solutions?" Say, "Now choose your solution and accomplish it." If the student makes a mistake, he or she will suffer the consequences, but at least will be aware of what those consequences are.

PUNCTUALITY—Being on Time or Ahead of Time for Any Scheduled Activity

Dayle can always sit in her preferred spot in class if she is early. By arriving on time or early, she can also study the layout of the room (who is there, what visuals are on the wall or board) so that she is in a better position to anticipate what will happen.

Suggestions: Assign a seat to the person with a learning disability. Organize the activities to take place so that it is clear from the beginning of the class or activity what is going to happen. Either tell the class members the sequence of events or write a schedule on an overhead projector or the blackboard. Use only key words.

PUNCTUATION—The Knowledge of Punctuation in Written Language and How to Use It When Writing

Individuals with written-language problems often have difficulties knowing how and when to use punctuation in their written materials. The rules do not make sense to them because they find the rules to be abstract, much the same way they find individual letters of the alphabet to be meaningless. Correct punctuation provides clarity of written work in order that the reader can interpret the work as the writer meant. Since punctuation is very difficult for many individuals with learning disabilities, it is instructive to read what Dayle has to say about the topic and the strategies she has found useful.

PUNCTUATION ACCORDING TO DAYLE

What does *punctuation* mean? I am sure most of you know the traditional meaning of this word. But let me give you a different perspective. With this new perspective there will only be a period (.), a comma (,), an exclamation point (!), a question mark (?), and quotation marks (" "). The use of any other mark on the page will be incorrect.

Let me now give you the rules for the use of the above punctuation.

- Comma—use this when you have read what you have written, and you pause. (Where you breathe is where you put the comma.)
- Exclamation point—use this when you are angry or you want to drive home a point.
- Question mark—use this when someone is asking a question.
- Quotation marks—use these when it sounds like someone is talking.
- Period—use this liberally at the end of a thought, or when you're in doubt of what you should use.

Following are the rules for using a grammar-check program on your computer. The grammar check looks much like the spell checker. A message box will appear with a message written you may be unable to decipher. Disregard this message. Return to the text and first shorten your sentence by using a period somewhere about the middle of your long line of words, cutting it into two shorter sentences. Try the grammar check again. If the message is still there, keep changing the words and placing periods in what feels like logical places until the message disappears. You then know everything is okay.

I would tell you what the traditional meaning of *punctuation* is, but, I have never exactly understood what it means. While I was in school, I was sure that English teachers made up special codes that only they understood. For years I thought I didn't like English teachers, but then I realized I just didn't like what they taught. If I started to understand what they were talking about, their reply would be, "But this is an exception to the rule." Later, I would find there were exceptions to the exceptions. I haven't yet addressed the whole issue of paragraphs, salutations, and all the other secret codes. But let me give you a secret of my own. If you have to do a lot of writing, find samples you especially like and keep copies. When you have to write something, use the sample and change the words. Be sure to keep all the marks in the same places, and read what you've written, out loud. Then have someone proofread your writing. This is the best advice I can give to those of you who have no idea what punctuation is all about. If I could change this strange way of communicating, I would. But I had to make up my own code. For all the English teachers who have tried to share the secret code with me, I thank you. For those of you who are like me, I hope my secret will assist you in your communication process. I say, "Good luck to you."

READING—Try a Variety of Reading Approaches

Like many individuals with learning disabilities, Dayle will never be an excellent reader. At the completion of her Ph.D. program, she will still read at approximately a high school level when tested on a common reading-assessment instrument. Attempts have been made to teach her using phonics approaches, whole language approaches, and several combinations of the two. Now, she reports, she uses some of each approach as she decodes and understands written material. For Dayle, knowing a number of approaches to reading has allowed her to read well enough to tackle very difficult reading. When she finds the demands of the reading process too great, she uses one of her other strategies (such as engaging friends who have read all the information in a discussion of the material) in addition to her own reading.

Suggestions: Try each reading approach until you are certain that it is not going to result in appropriate reading skills. Then try other approaches in the same manner. Sometimes, a return to an earlier approach may work better than it did originally. It is important to stay with one approach until it is clear that it is not going to work well, at least at this time. Continuing to use a method that leads to failure results in a student who loses all interest in trying to learn to read.

Help the individual with a learning disability find other ways to learn from written information. Use discussions of the material, tapes of books, films of the material, and so forth. Use magazines and newspapers such as *Reader's Digest* and *USA Today,* since they use relatively short passages but offer information that is current and entertaining. Encourage the individual gaining information from these abbreviated reading sources to discuss what they have read with others and to use broadcasts from National Public Radio and television to further their knowledge on a subject.

With an older individual who does not read, try the services of the region's literacy program.

SOCIAL/EMOTIONAL (NONVERBAL CUES)—Learning to Anticipate How a Person Is Feeling and/or Behaving by Observing Nonverbal Cues

For a person who does not read or write well, it can be extremely helpful to learn what is meant by certain facial expressions, ways of standing and walking, arm gestures, type of clothing worn, and so forth. Dayle has learned to predict what each of these cues means, and is able to prepare accordingly. If a teacher always stands in a certain place before asking questions of the class, if a specific facial expression or stance means anger, when the way a person walks indicates how he or she feels, it is very helpful to know the cues.

Suggestions: Use pictures or simulations of facial expressions. Discuss with the student(s) what each expression might mean.

Role play all sorts of nonverbal communication traits and discuss possible meanings and ways to anticipate what is coming next.

SPELLING—Strategies for Coping

People with learning disabilities are often plagued with spelling difficulties. Since over 50 percent of English spellings are irregular or exceptions to grammatical rules, it is not surprising that someone with a learning disability will have trouble mastering spelling. In spite of Dayle's excellent visual memory, she can't remember the spelling of words she sees. When she is asked to spell a word such as *people*, she sees a group of people instead of the word. When asked to spell *peculiar*, Dayle recalls a scene or situation that was peculiar in some way, instead of the letters that make up the word. She tries to use what she knows about phonics to put words together, but this fails because of the irregularity of spelling in the English language. Sometimes, her visual memory serves her well and she spells an abstract word such as *when* correctly, sometimes she spells it as *wen*. Homonyms—words that sound the same but are spelled differently—are almost impossible for Dayle and individuals like her to figure out. Since spelling is a basic language skill, poor spellers must find a way to cope with the problem.

Suggestions: Use a spell-check program on a computer. If the program does not account for issues of word usage—such as homonyms—have someone proofread the writing as well.

Purchase an electronic speller or a Franklin computer. The advantage of the Franklin computer is that it includes a spell-check program, a thesaurus, and a dictionary.

Use a thesaurus: Dayle has found this to be a very useful tool because it allows her to look up a synonym of the word she can spell and then find the spelling of the word she wants. For instance, if Dayle cannot spell *enormous,* she can look up *big* in the thesaurus and find *enormous* listed.

SUPPORT SYSTEM—Developing a Support System

Friends, family, teachers can offer advice, proofread, provide constructive criticism and praise, and validate the value of the person with the learning disability. All people need to know that they are valuable, that they have something to offer society, and that someone cares about what happens to them. The person with a learning disability seems even needier because his or her weaknesses lie in academic and social areas which have been judged by society to be basic to success. It is very easy for a person with poor reading, writing, math, speaking, or personal interaction skills to feel hopeless and useless. It is easy to come to believe that these skills underlie almost everything one wants to do—follow written directions, maintain finances, obtain jobs, read to a child, and so forth. A system of support people can help the individual understand his or her strengths and offer suggestions for how to use those strengths to cope with weaknesses, like *telling* a child a wonderful story rather than reading it, or learning to use a computer to enhance writing skills.

Suggestions: Be available to help the individual with the learning disability analyze and solve problems. Offer support and advice, but do not try to solve the problem yourself or complete the task for the person. This leads to learned helplessness. Help the student understand and use her strengths.

Teach the individual how to use a thesaurus as an aid in spelling. (See the strategy on spelling.) Teach him or her how to use spell-check and grammar-check programs on the computer.

Offer to proofread written work. Offer suggestions, but do not rewrite the paper!

TELLING A STORY—Telling a Written Assignment as a Story

A person with a writing problem may use visualization and creativity strengths by "seeing" a written assignment as an interesting story to be told through a series of images that have personal meaning. This de-emphasizes the fearful awareness of spelling, punctuation, and grammar problems and frees the individual to move into a story-telling mode. Asking a person with a learning disability to talk about incidents in his or her own life, and feelings associated with those incidents, validates those incidents and feelings.

Suggestions: Tell the student that you want her to write, in story form, a description of an experience and her feelings about that experience. The first draft can be written in outline form or incomplete sentences. Communicate the point that the ideas come first, and the grammatical structure later. Then communicate that the ideas should be organized in sequence—beginning, middle, and end.

Once the individual has stated the ideas clearly, help him or her to work on the grammar. This can be done with the help of peer editors, conferencing with the teacher, friend, or parent, or a spelling and grammar checker on a computer.

When you receive a paper, read it aloud to the student, asking how it sounds, then make any changes suggested. You might eventually have an entire group of students try this same process and ask them to proofread each other's papers as a group.

TIME TELLING—The Skill That We Use
Daily to Organize Our Day and Our Activities

Telling time is as abstract as learning to read and many children with learning disabilities find the concept difficult (Lerner, 1993; Trumbull, 1976). When we consider that time on a clock merely represents the passage of activities somewhere else, we begin to realize how abstract the clock-reading skill actually is.

Suggestions: Use a digital timepiece. Since very young children are not developmentally ready to tell time, do not attempt to teach this skill too early. Children with learning disabilities learn to use a timepiece with understanding later than other children, often not until second or third grade.

TIREDNESS—See Chapter 6, Commentary

TRAVELING—Finding a Location One Has Never Visited

The person who cannot read quickly or who has trouble with directions or map reading can easily become disoriented. Being able to read and understand geographic directions is an essential part of life. Dayle is excellent at all the mechanics of driving. However, she cannot focus on those mechanics and the reading necessary to find her way at the same time. She cannot always rely on another person to take her to a new location.

Suggestions: Encourage the person to take the trip to the new location several days before the appointed day and time to avoid stress.

Draw a map, pointing out all the route changes and left–right turns ahead of time. In Dayle's situation, it is important that she actually sees the route and has someone tell her the directions to the new location.

Describe the route in terms of physical landmarks along the road. (For instance, "Turn at the big green house with white shutters," "Go past the Exxon station.")

VERSATILITY—Development of Academic or Nonacademic Strengths

The development of areas of strength, even if they appear to have nothing to do with academics, provides confidence for Dayle and other individuals with learning disabilities that they can be adequate in something. If her dreams of further academic work do not work out, she knows she can develop her carpentry skills into kitchen design or furniture making, or her artistry in photography into a career.

Suggestions: From early in life, provide children with learning disabilities with concrete projects that build on their interests. For instance, buy a camera, collect and press wild flowers, provide music lessons, find a carpenter mentor for him or her to work with. Work with the individual to plan step-by-step how he or she will undertake the project.

WRITING—The Ability to Communicate in Written Language

In most societies, skill in written language is a characteristic of the educated person. Much of communication requires these skills and, as a result, they are taught throughout the school years. Not only does an individual with poor writing skills have difficulty in school, most jobs require at least rudimentary writing skills.

Suggestions: Writing includes such topics as formation of letters, grammar, punctuation, spelling, vocabulary, sequencing, organization, and clarity of expression. An individual with a learning disability may have problems in one or several of these areas. Dayle has trouble with punctuation, spelling, and organization (see strategies for punctuation and spelling above). Her solutions for organization include making a careful outline of the topic and picturing in her mind the sequence of her story or research paper. Since she is so visual in her approach to learning, she often leaves out key descriptions and concepts in her writing, believing that the reader can visualize them just as she does. Reading her own written language aloud (or having someone read it to her) helps Dayle understand what she has omitted.

Practice through the years has probably had the most influence on the organization of Dayle's writing. The more an individual with a learning disability can be encouraged to write, the better. At first the written pieces should be very short; directions to someone's house, a children's story, letters to friends, and so forth.

Appendix B

REFERENCES

This section includes entries that we consider to be most useful to individuals who are working with people with learning disabilities and to those people who themselves have a learning disability. The references are divided into professional books, books with popular appeal, videotapes, and organizations. Each reference is annotated so that you can choose those that interest you. Many of the entries include useful bibliographies and some include valuable appendices.

PROFESSIONAL BOOKS

Bos, C.S., & Vaughn, S. (1994). *Strategies for teaching students with learning and behavior problems.* (2nd ed.) Needham Heights, MA: Allyn & Bacon.

This very readable textbook includes a chapter on socialization and computer-assisted instruction for children and adolescents with learning disabilities. There is an excellent appendix on instructional activities that provides a number of realistic activities useful to teachers and parents.

Gregg, N., Hoy & Gay, A.F. (1995, Ed.) *Adults with learning disabilities: Theoretical & practical perspectives.* New York: The Guilford Press.

This edited book contains an excellent group of readings on adults with learning disabilities. The problems this group of people experience are noted, and recent research cited to explain what is known about social and affective adjustment, literacy problems, sociocultural issues, and employment in the individual with a learning disability. The reader who is interested in an up-to-date survey of current research and thinking on adults with learning disabilities will find this book very valuable.

Kotilak, R. (1996). *Inside the brain.* Kansas City, MO: Andrews and McMeel.

This factual book is easy to read, describing the structure of the brain, the effects of damage to the brain, and the repair and renewal of this organ. Chapter topics include the effects of violence and stress, alcohol, memory and brain processing, and the effects of stroke and spinal cord damage on children's brains.

Kurtz, L.A., Dowrick, P.W., Levy, S.E., & Batshaw, M.L. (1996). *Handbook of developmental disabilities: Resources for interdisciplinary care.* Baltimore, MD: Aspen.

This is an excellent resource for professionals working with individuals who have developmental disabilities. Descriptions of the disabilities, resources, parent and professional issues, education, and much more are included in this very comprehensive book.

Lerner, J. (1993). *Learning disabilities.* (6th ed.) Boston: Houghton Mifflin Co.

This classic text on learning disabilities provides an excellent overview of the field of learning disabilities, from its foundation to the present. It includes a review of the history, theories, and practices in the field. The appendices include a case study used to demonstrate the stages of the assessment–teaching process, an annotated list of tests useful in assessing students with learning disabilities, and a directory including the addresses of publishers and organization.

Levine, Mel. (1990). *Keeping a head in school.* Cambridge, MA: Educators Publishing Service, Inc.

This book is written for preadolescents and adolescents who want to understand learning disorders from a personal perspective. Students' stories are interspersed with text by Dr. Levine that explains brain functioning, the acquisition of academic skills, and social problems that commonly accompany learning problems. Many practical strategies are included. Teachers, as well as students, will find this book readable and a useful basis for a discussion of what it means to have a learning disorder.

Levine, Mel. (1993). *All kinds of minds.* Cambridge, MA: Educators Publishing Service, Inc.

In this book for school-age children, Dr. Levine uses case studies and real kids to tell their own stories of what it is like to have a variety of learning disorders. In addition to the stories, there are lots of suggestions for what teachers can do to help these students and what students can do to help themselves. The book is written with language and script that can be read by the children themselves or to a group of children by a teacher or parent.

Levine, Mel. (1994). *Educational care: A system for understanding and helping children with learning problems at home and in school.* Cambridge, MA: Educators Publishing Service, Inc.

Both teachers and parents will find this a valuable text for helping them understand the different types of learning disorders. There is a great deal of helpful and up-to-date information written in layman's language. Every chapter includes strategies for helping teachers and parents work successfully with the child. The appendices include planning and interview formats that may be used as aids in informal assessment. Also included are short sections on resources for parents, children, and teachers, and a reading list with short descriptions of the books and articles.

Mercer, C.D. & Mercer, A.R. (1993). *Teaching students with learning problems.* (4th ed.) New York: Macmillan.

This text contains many suggestions for instructional activities and informal assessment of skills. The book includes a section on teaching students at the secondary school level and does a good job throughout in its discussion of elementary and high school students with learning problems. An excellent appendix includes scope and sequence skills lists in math, reading, spelling, handwriting, and written expression. These lists include those skills generally learned by the end of the sixth grade but are useful in the determination of the sequence of skills learned in any of the academic areas in which a student at any grade level is having problems.

Turnbull, A.P. & Turnbull, H.R., III (1990). *Families, professionals and exceptionality: A special partnership.* (2nd ed.) Columbus, OH: Merrill.

This helpful book focuses on the relationship between professionals and families. Included are concrete ideas about working together successfully on behalf of the child with a disability. Legal issues that have an impact on children with disabilities and their families are discussed.

Wallach, G.P. & Butler, K.G. (1994). *Language learning disabilities in school-age children and adolescents.* New York: Macmillan.

This textbook deals with children who have language-based learning disabilities. Discussed are language problems related to learning disabilities, curricula-based assessment, and strategies for use in the classroom.

Wigg, E.H. & Semel, E.M. (1984). *Language assessment and intervention for the learning disabled.* (2nd ed.) Columbus, OH: Merrill.

Although this book is somewhat dated, it is a wonderful source of ideas for teachers to use in the classroom. It helps professionals understand what a language-based learning disability is and how to address it.

POPULAR BOOKS

Lee, C. & Jackson, P. (1992). *Faking it: A look into the mind of a creative learner.* Portsmouth, NH: Heinemann.

Lelewer, N. (1994). *Something's not right.* Acton, MA: VanderWyk & Burnham.

This is a heart-warming autobiography about a family of four children, three of whom had learning disabilities. The reader clearly understands the difficulties of raising the children, especially when the dyslexic author is also the children's mother. The book speaks to teachers and parents who find themselves trying to meet the needs of such children.

MacCracken, M. (1986). *Turnabout children.* New York: Signet.

The author of *A Circle of Children,* the story of a teacher who used her skills to help children with severe emotional disabilities, again demonstrates her teaching and caring skills in this book about students with learning disabilities.

Orlansky, M.D. & Heward, W.L. (1981). *Voices: Interviews with handicapped people*. Columbus, OH: Merrill.

An interesting collection of stories told by individuals with various types of disabilities. One of the best ways to understand what it is like to have a disability is to listen to someone who lives with one on a daily basis.

Roby, C. (1994). *When learning is tough*. Morton Grove, IL: Albert Whitman & Co.

Subtitled "kids talk about their learning disabilities," this book cites the individual stories of several children and adolescents with learning disabilities. The individuals talk about their learning problems and what it feels like to have a disability. This is a good introduction for children to help them understand themselves and others.

ORGANIZATIONS

AHEAD (Association on Higher Education and Disability), PO Box 21192, Columbus, OH 43221-0192. (614) 488-4972

A professional organization for educators committed to promoting full participation of individuals with disabilities in college. The organization maintains a large number of publications regarding post-secondary education for persons with disabilities.

CEC (Council for Exceptional Children), 1920 Association Dr., Reston, VA 22091

CHADD (Children with Attention Deficit Disorder), 499 Northwest 70th Ave., Suite 308, Plantation, FL 33317

Deveroux Foundation, Devon, PA 19333

HEATH National Resources Center, American Council on Education, One Dupont Circle, Suite 800, Washington, DC 20036-1193. (800) 544-3284

National clearinghouse on post-secondary education for individuals with disabilities.

International Reading Association, 800 Barksdale Rd., Newark, DE 19711

LDA (Learning Disabilities Association), 4156 Library Rd., Pittsburgh, PA 15234-1349. (412) 341-1515

A national organization devoted to defining and finding solutions for the broad spectrum of learning disabilities.

Learning Disabilities Association of America, 4156 Library Road, Pittsburgh, PA 15234-1349. (412) 341-1515 or (412) 341-8077

National Education Association Publications, 1201 16th St. NW, Washington, DC 20036

NCLD (National Center for Learning Disabilities), 381 Park Avenue, New York, NY 10016. (212) 545-7510

NCLD is an organization committed to improving the lives of those affected by learning disabilities. NCLD provides services and conducts programs nationwide, benefiting children and adults, their families, teachers, and other professionals. NCLD provides the latest information on learning disabilities and local resources to parents, professionals, employers, and others dealing with learning disabilities. NCLD's annual publication is *Their World.*

Orton Dyslexia Society, Chester Building, Suite 382, 8600 La Salle Road, Baltimore, MD 21286-2044. (800) 222-3123/(410) 296-0232

Provides information on dyslexia, hosts national and local conferences, publishes a professional journal (*Annals of Dyslexia*), as well as a newsletter (*Perspectives*).

Recording for the Blind and Dyslexic, The Anne T. MacDonald Center, 20 Roszel Road, Princeton, NJ 08540. (800) 221-4792

Provides educational and professional books in accessible media format to people with print disabilities. This organization has an extensive, free library of books on audiocassette covering a wide range of subjects and academic levels. Services are available to persons with a verified visual, physical, or specific learning disability that substantially limits reading.

UCLA Intervention Program for Handicapped Children, 1000 Veteran Ave., Room 23-10, Los Angeles, CA 90024

University of Connecticut Postsecondary Disability Technical Assistance Center, A.J. Pappanikou Center on Special Education and Rehabilitation, The University of Connecticut, U-64, 249 Glenbrook Road Storrs, CT 06269-2064. (860) 486-0163/(860) 486-0273

VIDEOTAPES

Many of the videotapes listed here are available from the Connecticut Postsecondary Disability Technical Assistance Center of the A.J. Pappanikou Center on Special Education & Rehabilitation, University of Connecticut. Phone: (860) 486-0273/0163. The descriptions of those films were prepared by the Center.

Coping with Learning Disabilities. Contact: Films for the Humanities, Inc., Box 2053, Princeton, NJ 08543-2053. (800) 257-5126

This videotape looks at people with learning disabilities and how they cope. Adults with learning disabilities reveal the difficulties they have faced, how they are challenging attitudes and responses that focus on their difficulties rather than on their potential, and how they are now taking charge of their lives.

Degrees of Success. Contact: NYU Access to Learning, 566 LaGuardia Pl., Room 701, New York, NY 10012. (212) 998-4978

Six students with learning disabilities from a variety of post-secondary settings describe their personal experiences. Obstacles they encountered such as low self-esteem, low expectations by teachers in secondary school, and social isolation are shared. Students describe how they found the inner strength to overcome their disabilities and the perceptions of others. They discuss the importance of understanding their own learning styles and unique needs and finding the best fit between them and the post-secondary institution that they select.

Dyslexia: Diagnosis and Therapy. Contact: Films for the Humanities, Inc., Box 2053, Princeton, NJ 08543-2053. (800) 257-5126

This program features eight children and adults of different ages who have been affected by dyslexia. It shows the relief that diagnosis brings and underscores the importance of early recognition. The program stresses that teachers and parents are uniquely placed to recognize the

signs of dyslexia, and alerts them to symptoms and the need for special-
ized guidance.

How Difficult Can This Be? Understanding Learning Disabilities. Contact:
Richard Lavoi, The Public Broadcasting Service, PBS Home Video,
WETA-TV, Washington, D.C.

This sixty-minute film has helped many teachers, young students, and
pre-service teachers understand what it means to have a learning disability. R. Lavoi is a powerful speaker who "transforms" each member of his
audience into a person with a learning disability. The result is a very effective film that has helped many people understand just what this disability
is and how it feels to go through school with a learning disability.

In Their Own Words. Contact: Project Extra, General College, University of
Minnesota, 140 Appleby Hall, 128 Pleasant St. S.E., Minneapolis, MN,
55455. (612) 625-5366

This videotape and guide (available with and without closed captioning)
was designed for parents, educators, agency providers, and students with
disabilities to assist them in the understanding of transition from adoles-
cence to adulthood. The students featured in this video program were
selected by the project staff because they demonstrated a successful transition from high school to post-secondary education setting. The goal of
the program was to help teachers, students, families, and adult service
providers increase their awareness and knowledge of the transition process for students who have disabilities.

*Last One Picked . . . First One Picked On: Learning Disabilities and Social
Skills.* Contact: Richard Lavoi, The Public Broadcasting Service, PBS
Home Video, WETA-TV, Washington, D.C.

This film addresses the social problems children with learning disabilities
often have and offers strategies for overcoming them. Lavoi narrates the
film and helps his audience understand how social problems and learning
disabilities can be related. This video is excellent for teachers and parents.

Learning Disabilities: Coping in College. Contact: Assistant Director, Handicapped Student Services, Wright State University, Dayton, OH 45435.
(513) 873-2140

This videotape presentation focuses on four students with learning disabilities at Wright State University. The students discuss the academic and
social issues related to their learning disabilities that they face in the college

setting. A situational enactment presented by a faculty member and a student with learning disability depicts inappropriate and appropriate ways to approach a professor to discuss the students' learning disability and the needed accommodations. The formation of a support group by students is viewed as the discussion focuses on their problems and peer recommendations for resolution. The students share personal compensation techniques and the accommodations they have requested for their course work. The video presents information on the services available to students with learning disabilities at Wright State University. A discussion guide is available.

Learning Disabilities in College: A Time for Self-Advocacy. Contact: Julie Geis, Learning Disabilities Project, University of Nebraska, 204H Barkley Memorial Center, Lincoln, NE 68583-0731. (404) 472-5503/5497

This videotape produced by the LD Talents project at the University of Nebraska consists of a panel of four college students who discuss their learning disabilities with moderator Julie Geis. Among the issues addressed are: academic problems students encountered because of their learning disabilities, suggestions for describing handicaps to instructors, experiences with test taking, and effects of the students' disabilities on their social lives. The discussion ends with a summary of important points to consider when working with students who have learning disabilities. Although there are some technical sound fluctuation problems with this tape, it offers useful information for both students with learning disabilities and service providers at post-secondary institutions.

Learning Disabilities in Higher Education. Contact: Office of Student Affairs, 237 Leavey Center, Georgetown University, Washington, DC 20057. (202) 687-6985

This video, written and produced at Georgetown University, presents the experiences of an accomplished faculty member with dyslexia and those of a student needing assessment to determine if a learning disability exists. The video describes the assistance the university provides to faculty and students regarding policies and procedures and the role of advocacy in working with students with learning disabilities.

Marketing Your Disability. Contact: Neil L. Cook, Editor, McBurney Resource Center, University of Wisconsin–Madison, 905 University Avenue, Madison, Wisconsin 53715. (608) 263-2741

This videotape, designed to assist job applicants with interviewing, opens with two businesspeople discussing some real-world problems surrounding the hiring of qualified employees. One problem addressed is that prospective applicants need to be able to integrate their job skills and qualifications in terms of some knowledge of the work world and general employment issues. The conversation further reveals that they have interviewed the same disabled college graduate, but with decidedly different outcomes. Jim Sperry, the applicant with a disability, is observed in two interviews. In the first interview, he responds weakly and inappropriately to most of the questions and violates several basic rules of job applicant conduct. Upon seeing his performance, we can see why Jim does not get the job. In the second interview, Jim presents his qualifications for the job, and we see a demonstration of more appropriate and positive behaviors. A summary highlights the main differences between the two interviews.

Part of the Team: People with Disabilities in the Workforce. Contact: National Easter Seals Society, Communications Dept., 70 East Lake St., Chicago, Illinois, 60601. (312) 726-6200 (phone) or (312) 726-4258 (TDD)

This video was produced as a public service by the IBM Corporation in cooperation with the National Easter Seal Society and the Work Environment and Technology Committee of the President's Committee on Employment of People with Disabilities. This video introduces you to eight managers and supervisors who know first-hand about working with people with disabilities as well as ten people with different kinds of disabilities. *Part of the Team* is valuable for awareness training on diversity in the workforce, and addressing questions about supervising people with disabilities. The video also provides information on whom to call for free assistance on hiring and accommodating people with disabilities.

Succeeding in the Workplace: Attention Deficit Disorders and Learning Disabilities in the Workplace: A Guide for Success. Contact: JKL Communications, P.O. Box 40157, Washington, DC 20016. (202) 223-5097

This career-planning program is now presented in two videotapes.
Tape 1: The first video is comprehensive, covering medical, legal, work accommodations, and personal strategies to promote success for individuals with learning disabilities and attention deficit disorder in the workplace. Additionally, this video includes the personal stories and strategies of those who have struggled with these hidden disabilities.
Tape 2: The second video is an overview of workplace issues and legal aspects. Fast paced and informative, it promotes awareness and understanding of the subject and includes personal stories. It is designed for

individuals with ADD or learning disabilities, their families, employers, coworkers, professionals, colleges, support groups, and libraries.

Yes We Can. Contact: Project Assist, Roseman 2019, Whitewater, WI 53109. (414) 471-4788

This is a panel discussion of students from Project Assist, a college support program for students with learning disabilities. The students share problems and successes they have faced throughout their educational careers. Students discuss the differences between high school and college, highlighting the emphasis on student responsibility and independence. Common themes throughout the discussion are problems with time management, a need for self-discipline, a need to seek help, and a need to believe in oneself.

Bibliography

Ariel, A. (1992). *Education of children and adolescents with learning disabilities.* New York: Merrill/Macmillan.

Bernstein, D. & Tiegermann, D. (1993). *Language and communication disorders.* (3rd. ed.) New York: Merrill/Macmillan.

Bloom, L. & Lahey, M. (1978). *Language disorders and language development.* New York: Macmillan.

Chomsky, N. (1957). *Syntactic structures.* The Hague: Mouton.

Gerber, P.J. & Reiff, H.B. (1991). *Speaking for themselves: Ethnographic interviews with adults with learning disabilities.* Ann Arbor, MI: University of Michigan Press.

IDEA (Individuals with Disabilities Education Act) (1990). Reauthorization of Public Law 94–142, the education for all handicapped children act.

Lerner, J. (1993). *Learning Disabilities.* (6th ed.) Boston: Houghton Mifflin Co.

Ryan, A. & Price, L. (1992). Adults with learning disabilities in 1990s. *Intervention, 9,* 6–20.

Trumbull, V. (1976). "Piaget time concepts in L.D. children." Unpublished dissertation. University of Virginia.

About the Authors

Dayle Upham began her course work at Keene State College in 1984. In 1986, she graduated with honors, certified to teach elementary and special education. Two years later, Dayle earned a master's degree in special education, excelling with a 3.6 grade point average.

For the following two years, Dayle taught junior high age students in Swanzey, New Hampshire, and began teaching her students how to develop strategies for coping with academic, social, and emotional problems. While studying for her PhD in special education at the University of Connecticut, Dayle worked with college age students with learning disabilities. Currently, Dayle is touching and teaching lives as an assistant professor of special education at the University of Wisconsin at Stephens Point.

Virginia H. Trumbull, Ed.D., is a professor of special education at Keene State College in Keene, New Hampshire. She arrived at the college in 1974 after completing her doctoral studies in learning and communication disabilities at the University of Virginia. Prior to her faculty position, Dr. Trumbull initiated and developed the Learning Disability Program in Windham Southeast Supervisory Union, Brattleboro, Vermont. This followed several years of teaching children and adolescents with special needs, classroom teaching in Biology and Ecology, and working as a specialist in outdoor education.

Dr. Trumbull readily admits that she has learned most of what she knows about learning disabilities from the students she has taught, their parents, and their teachers. Among her students was Dayle Upham.